# Lincoln's Deathbed in Art and Memory

## The "Rubber Room" Phenomenon

Harold Holzer and Frank J. Williams

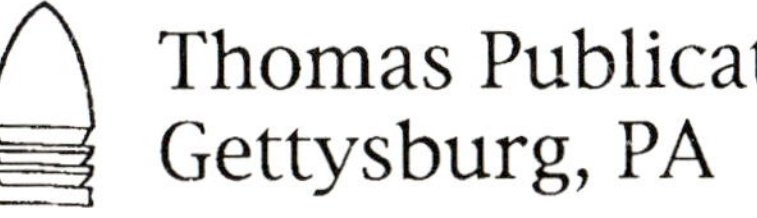

Thomas Publications
Gettysburg, PA 17325

Printed and bound in the United States of America

Published by THOMAS PUBLICATIONS
P.O. Box 3031
Gettysburg, Pa. 17325



ISBN-1-57747-028-1

Cover design by Ryan C. Stouch

Front cover illustration by Max Rosenthal, *The Last Moments of Abraham Lincoln, President of the United States.* Hand-colored lithograph published in Philadelphia, 1865, courtesy of The Lincoln Museum, Fort Wayne, Indiana.

Back cover illustrations: (left) *Harper's Weekly* May 6, 1865; (right) United States Army Military History Institute, Carlisle, PA.

*To Meg—*

*Fellow traveler on the Lincoln trail*

# CONTENTS

# FOREWORD

by Dwight T. Pitcaithley
*Chief Historian, National Park Service*

For historians and critical readers of history who value the power and significance of graphic evidence in intellectually and physically re-creating and interpreting the past, *Lincoln's Deathbed in Art and Memory: The "Rubber Room" Phenomenon* provides a chronology of artistic efforts to interpret the deathbed scene, as well as a thoughtful, insightful, and entertaining analysis of those images. The writers have devoted decades of scholarship to the study of Lincoln and his times and the results of that collective effort are evident throughout this brief study.

For those who manage and interpret historic properties, descriptions of past appearance and condition are crucial to preservation and education programs. Preservationists mine diaries, letters, official records, archives, attics, photographs and other graphic representations to determine how a house, building, or landscape may have appeared at some point in history. They sift through the evidence, reconcile (or attempt to reconcile) conflicting evidence, and draw conclusions to the best of their abilities knowing that in most instances, the historical record is not complete. Since the mid-nineteenth century, photography has provided graphic evidence of historic places although, as with those taken in the aftermath of the Battle of Gettysburg, even photographic evidence can be manipulated.

In situations when the photographic record is incomplete or altogether absent, artists' renderings, lithographs, etchings, and the like can prove invaluable for interpreting the actual appearance of a specific place. Even more than with photographs, however, the careful researcher must be aware of the degree to which artistic license or bias must be taken into consideration when evaluating this form of graphic evidence. Artistic renderings of the small room in which Abraham Lincoln died present an example of the multiple and conflicting images historians can encounter. In the days and months following the death of Lincoln, presses published and republished varying images of the death scene being accurate when convenient, but never hesitating to embellish when deemed commercially expedient. The "Rubber Room" as Harold Holzer and Frank Williams aptly call it, is in fact a narrow room to the rear of the Petersen House, the "House Where Lincoln Died," that measures but nine by seventeen feet.

This study provides readers with fascinating details about the events surrounding the deathbed vigil of April 14 and 15, 1865 and about art and the construction of history. But most importantly, after reading this information, what they thought they knew about that small room and the historical recreation of that somber scene will never be the same. And therein lies the value of this study.

# INTRODUCTION

Modern research into the American presidency suggests that the death of a sitting chief executive invariably generates a deep and enduring impact on the citizenry. Personal shock quickly gives way to public anxiety, fueled by a bombardment of news and pictures of the tragedy that keep nightmarish memories vividly and profoundly alive. Americans who live through such traumas are virtually lurched from the abyss of political apathy. By contrast, deaths of other leaders, political and national alike, seem to inspire only momentary ripples in the public consciousness.[1]

The pervasive mourning triggered by the violent death of incumbent presidents—from Lincoln to Garfield to McKinley to Kennedy—proves that the resident of the White House occupies a unique place in the collective American psyche. Presidents are more than authority figures; they are the living "fathers" of their country.[2] Sometimes the separation between family and state blurs. After all, when would-be assassin Lynette "Squeaky" Fromme pointed her pistol at Gerald Ford, she may have been taking aim not only at a president, but at a middle-class father who had ousted her from her family home.[3]

The death of a president can be a uniquely potent rite of passage for a polity. John F. Kennedy's murder in 1963 froze the chief executive as an eternal youth in national memory, and compelled Americans who lived through his death to leave their own youth and innocence behind. The aching sense of loss generated by that assassination may help explain why Kennedy's brief time in office has been so treasured, for so long, by so much of the American public, a reverence that many historians judge to be of proportion to Kennedy's accomplishments.[4]

The first—and still the most wrenching—of these national calamities was the murder of Abraham Lincoln only days after the Union had achieved victory in the long and bloody Civil War.

Lincoln died at the successful conclusion of an Armageddon that finally reconciled the living nations' values with those enshrined in the Declaration of Independence, so mass shock and mourning were surely not surprising. But Lincoln also died generations before the age of live television, years before photographs could even be reproduced in newspapers. The vast majority of his people never saw Lincoln in the flesh, and were totally unfamiliar with the theater where he was shot, or the house where he died. Yet his assassination made mourners out of countless Americans who were able to visualize the scenes of his martyrdom and death. They did so through the vastly under-appreciated medium of popular art.

The seemingly primitive depictions of Abraham Lincoln's final moments that have so often been dismissed by modern observers assumed in their own day the status of holy icons. That is not to say that they were all dependably researched, skillfully crafted, or free of commercial motivation. In fact, few could claim such status. The somber death scene that ended Abraham Lincoln's life offered to visual artists the same transcendent opportunity to preserve a defining historical moment that peace and re-union had afforded Lincoln himself in life. Many of the artists failed where Lincoln had succeeded.

But even if most pictorial representations of Lincoln's death lacked realism and good draftsmanship, all of them—paintings, popular prints, and photo-montages—deserve renewed appreciation today because of their staggering popularity at the time they were issued, and their decisive impact on popular culture and American collective memory. Artists, engravers, lithographers, and photographers produced their vast array of pictures in response to commercial demand, but their results confirmed, and may have influenced, Lincoln's status as the martyr of liberty. Through these pictures, today's Americans can open a window into the way 19th-century Americans learned about Abraham Lincoln's death, and came to respond to it as the defining event of their age.

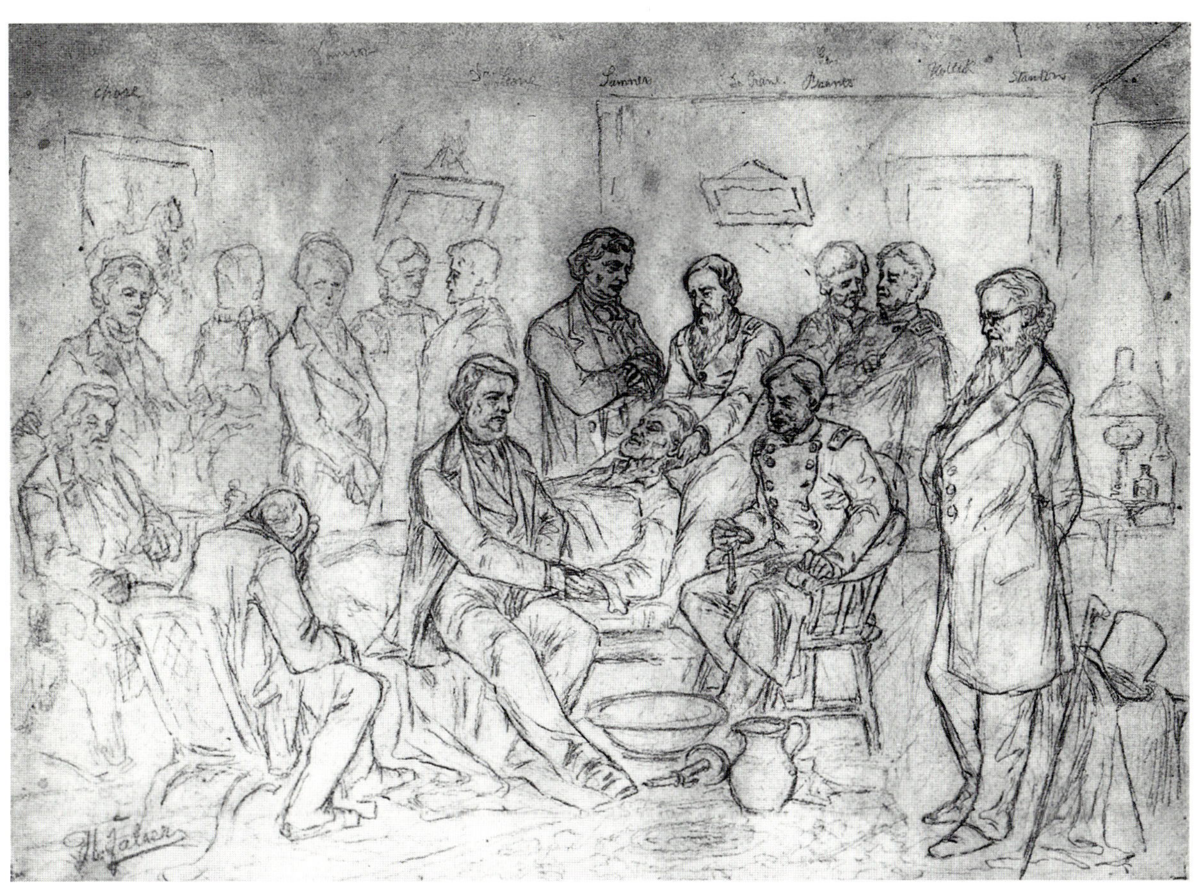

*Herman Faber,* **Deathbed of President Lincoln, April 15, 1865**. *This rarely seen sketch (see alternative Faber sketch, Figure 2) was made on the scene after the President's body was taken back to the White House. The people in the room were sketched from period photographs. The drawing is unusual because it shows the attending physicians actively working on Lincoln, a bowl and pitcher lying next to the bedside. Most deathbed scenes published later by engravers and lithographers suggested that eyewitnesses merely stood back reverently to await the great man's passing. But the sketch also launched a pattern of misrepresentation by significantly exaggerating the size of the death chamber. (National Museum of Health & Medicine)*

# FROM FORD'S THEATRE TO THE PETERSEN HOUSE

At one time, every school child knew the story. After the fatal shot was fired in Ford's Theatre, all was confusion. After he rushed into the president's box, Dr. Charles Leale, a 23-year-old assistant Army surgeon, ordered the president placed on the floor and examined the wounded chief executive. Finding blood on the back of Lincoln's head, Leale searched and found the hole made by John Wilkes Booth's attack. Concluding that the bullet was still in the president's brain, Leale realized the president had been mortally wounded. Quickly, he put his own mouth on that of the president and breathed into it. The president's labored breathing began again.

Some on the scene urged that the president be taken back to the White House, but Leale insisted that he could not survive the trip. It was then decided to move Lincoln to a dwelling nearby. At virtually the same moment, young Henry Safford, a tenant in William Petersen's house across from Ford's Theatre on Tenth Street, heard noises from the street, opened his window and shouted, "What's the matter?"[5]

"The President has been shot," came the answer. Going to the front door, Safford heard a voice call out, "Where shall we take him?" Safford cried, "Bring him in here." He watched the men bearing Lincoln struggle with the right angle of the steps. Commanded to "take me to your best room," Safford led the way to a small sleeping compartment, 9 1/2 by 17 feet, at the back of the first floor hall, occupied at the time by one William T. Clark, a soldier on leave who was not in his room at the time the president arrived.[6]

The president's 6'4" frame required that he be laid diagonally on the bed that Clark had been using. Lincoln's head was propped up so he could breathe more easily. His feet protruded from beneath the covers, as later described to artist Albert Berghaus by the displaced boarder, Willie Clark *(Figure 1)*.[7] Officials began gathering around the bedside, beginning a vigil later described to artist Hermann Faber, who sketched this scene only a few hours after Lincoln's death *(Figure 2)*.

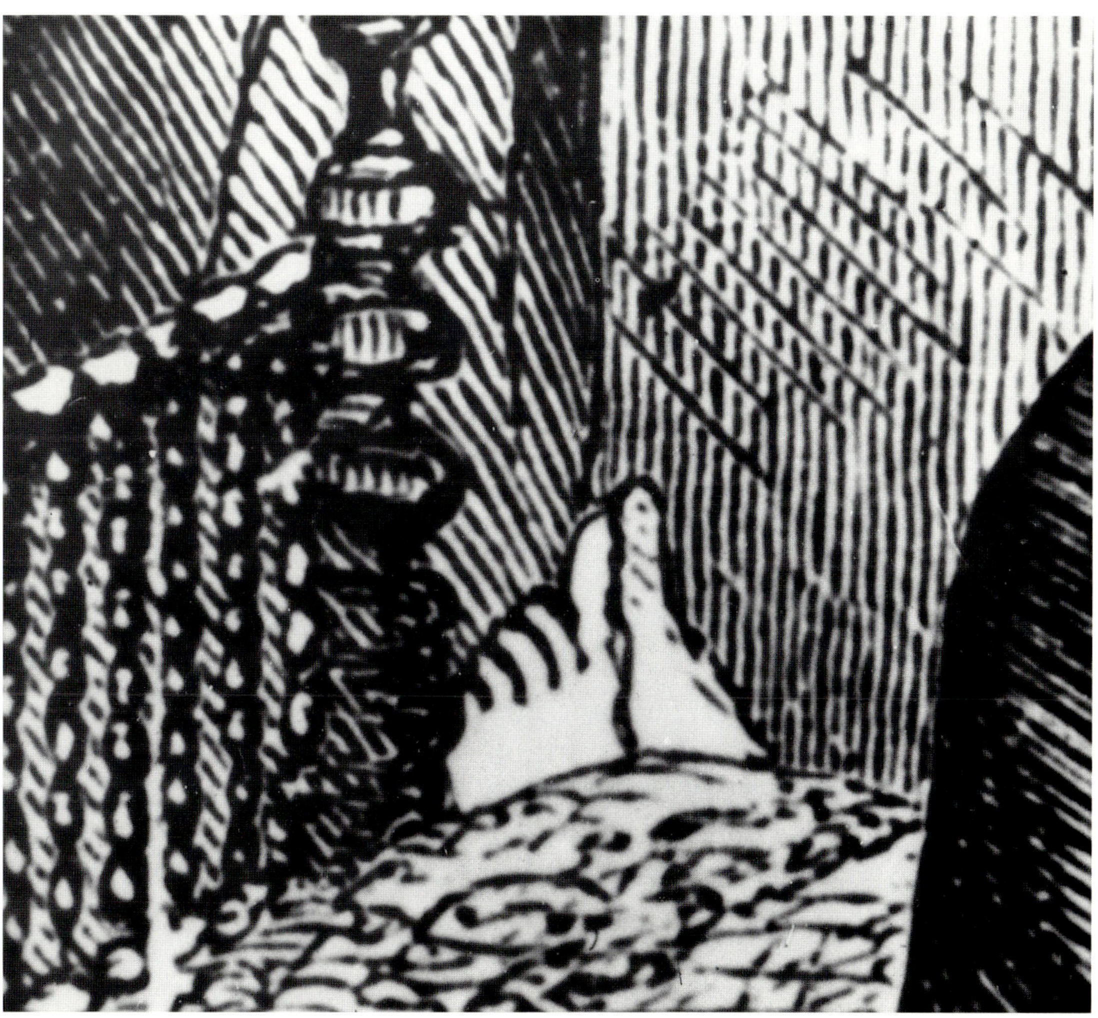

*Figure 1. Albert Berghaus,* **Lincoln's feet protruding from deathbed coverlet. Washington, 1865.** *This sketch was based on a description of the death scene by Petersen House boarder Willie Clark. (Ford's Theatre Collection)*

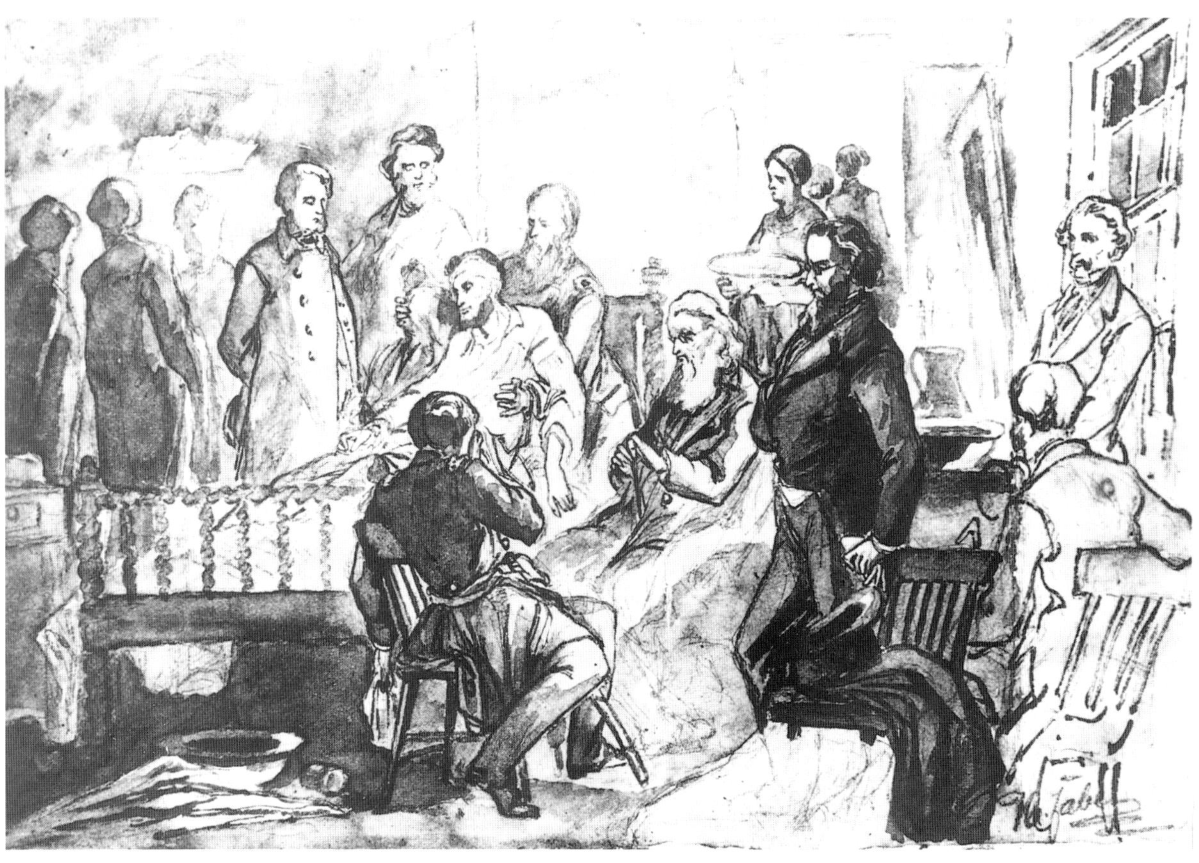

*Figure 2. Hermann Faber,* **The death of Lincoln. Washington, 1865**. *Sitting by the bedside is Secretary of the Navy Gideon Welles, and standing next to him, Secretary of War Edwin M. Stanton. This is the only rendering, contemporary or retrospective, that suggested that doctors had bandaged Lincoln's head wound. (Meserve-Kunhardt Collection)*

By this time, Dr. Joseph K. Barnes, the Surgeon General of the Army, had joined several other doctors at the scene. All they could do, however, was try to keep Lincoln warm, administer occasional stimulants, put the then-popular mustard plaster on his chest, and keep the wound open and free of blood clots to prevent pressure from building up inside his brain. In this condition, Lincoln lingered for almost nine excruciating hours before he drew his last breath at 7:22 the next morning, Saturday, April 15, 1865.[8]

Several times during the night, Mary Lincoln came into the death room for brief periods. Once, she threw herself on the bed beside her husband. Robert, their eldest son, either stood by his father's side or struggled to soothe his mother while Senator Charles

Sumner, in turn, comforted Robert. All manner of governmental personnel came and went throughout the night. In all, some 55 individuals visited the dying president's bedside—but not all at the same time, as some artists would later suggest in their interpretations of the scene. Secretary of War Edwin Stanton took charge. No one questioned his authority, even though Vice President Andrew Johnson made a brief call during the vigil. Stanton directed the search for Booth and his co-conspirators after the actor was identified as the assailant.[9]

At least that is what Americans read in the first editions of their morning newspapers. Beyond these sketchy details, almost any embellishment was deemed possible and, judging by the artistic results, believable to a gullible public hungry for visualizations of the tragic scene.

Even the circumstances surrounding Lincoln's removal from the theater to his deathbed across the street were suffused with controversy and eventually pictured differently by artists. Confusion begins with how Lincoln was "borne by loving hands,"[10] in the words of one painting of that frenzied scene. Some speculated that he was carried on a theater box partition. Others claimed he was carried by men holding him in their arms. From the accounts deemed more reliable, it is most likely that the president was transported on a flat board of some type. Who carried Lincoln from the theater? Surely fewer than the dozen eyewitnesses who later claimed the honor of removing the president.[11]

The artist Albert Berghaus later described the room where Lincoln died thusly: "The walls are covered with a brownish paper, figured with a white design. Its dimensions are about ten by fifteen feet. Some engravings and a photograph hang upon the walls.... The only furniture in the room was a bureau covered with crochet, a table, eight or nine plain chairs, and the bed upon which Mr. Lincoln lay when his spirit took its flight. The bedstead was a low walnut, with headboard from two to three feet high. The floor was carpeted with Brussels, considerably worn. Everything on the bed was stained with...blood...."[12]

The Lincoln death vigil centered, of course, on the deathbed itself. To an almost unnerving degree, the imagination, the emotion, and the memory of ordinary Americans hovered over what its citizens came to transform into a sacred spot. For its news value alone, it is small wonder that printmakers—America's engravers and lithographers—gravitated to it, as they had portrayed the deathbed scenes of the Father of our Country and Henry Clay, Lincoln's "beau ideal of a statesman."[13]

Lincoln's path to sainthood was further assured because he was assassinated on Good Friday, dying suddenly and violently, and not at home in bed as George Washington had in 1799. Printmakers seemed to believe that the public preferred its fallen leaders to die in places worthy of their exalted positions, and this perception encouraged them to enhance and embellish the place where Lincoln expired. They ignored, in large part, that the people recognized—and appreciated—the symmetry and humility consistent with greatness in a president who was born in a log cabin and who died in a simple boarding house.

# THE ARTISTS' "RUBBER ROOM"[14]

It was the lithographic firm of Currier and Ives that set the pace, if not the standard, with a deathbed print copyrighted on April 26, 1865.[15] While it ordinarily took at least three weeks to produce a Civil War-era print, Currier & Ives assassination and deathbed scenes were produced in only two short weeks—lightning speed at the time— comparable to today's instantaneous television news coverage of breaking events, and reflective of both the keen interest of the public and the marketing skills of the printmakers. First an artist had to sketch such a scene on paper, then produce a lithograph on stone. Once printed, Currier & Ives prints were hand colored, with a separate artist assigned to apply each tint. The prints were then placed on a clothes line to dry.[16]

Like most of the prints that soon flooded the marketplace, theirs showed a stoic and sterile Lincoln without a trace of pain or discomfort. There was no blood in these prints, and certainly not the swelling of Lincoln's eye visible by the morning of his death.[17] His surgeons typically were depicted as sitting stoically by his bedside, but not at work—as they really were—periodically removing blood clots from his wound and keeping him warm.[18]

Nor was Lincoln's wife depicted in the hysterical frenzy that in reality overtook her that night. Instead she was usually portrayed as a calm, resolute woman moving almost gracefully through the event, gowned as if for an inaugural ball.

What is surprising about Currier & Ives print is not its errors—some attributable to artistic license, like the insertion of little Tad Lincoln crying on his mother's lap *(Figure 3)*. Tad was in fact never brought to his father's bedside that night, even though Mary more than once expressed the irrational belief that her husband would awake if only he

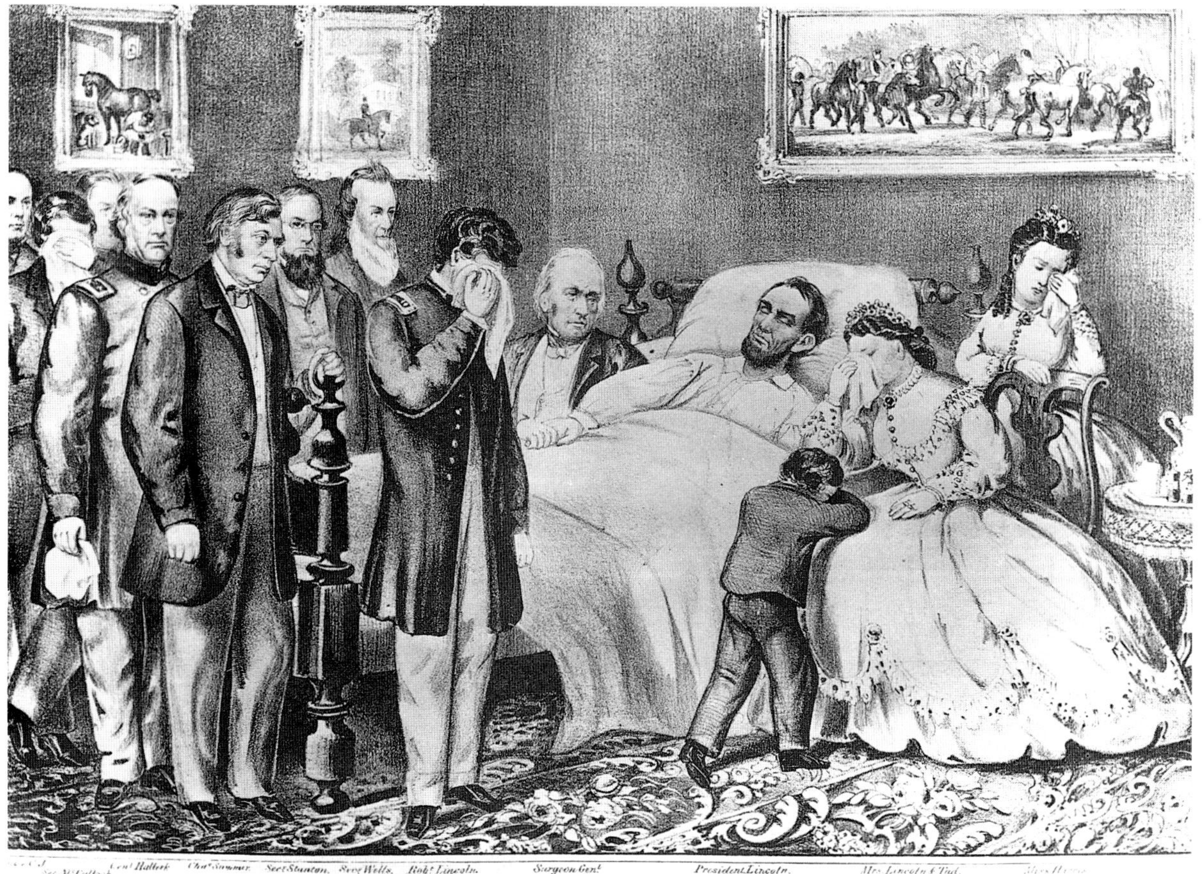


*Figure 3. Currier & Ives,* **Death of President Lincoln At Washington, D.C., April 15th, 1865 The Nation's Martyr.** *Lithograph, New York, 1865. First of three versions of the death room by America's best-known printmakers, included portraits of 12 eyewitnesses. (The Lincoln Museum, a part of the Lincoln National Corporation, Fort Wayne, Indiana)*

could hear Tad speak. What surprises is how many details the artist got right: particularly the print within the print on the wall in back of the deathbed. Many printmakers not only knew that the engraving of *The Village Blacksmith* hung in Lincoln's death room, but took pains to draw it in their scenes as well *(Figure 4).*

Most printmakers proved unaware—or unwilling to accept—the modest size of the death chamber itself, giving rise in popular art to what assassination expert Lesley A. Leonard has aptly called the "rubber room" phenomenon. In successive prints,

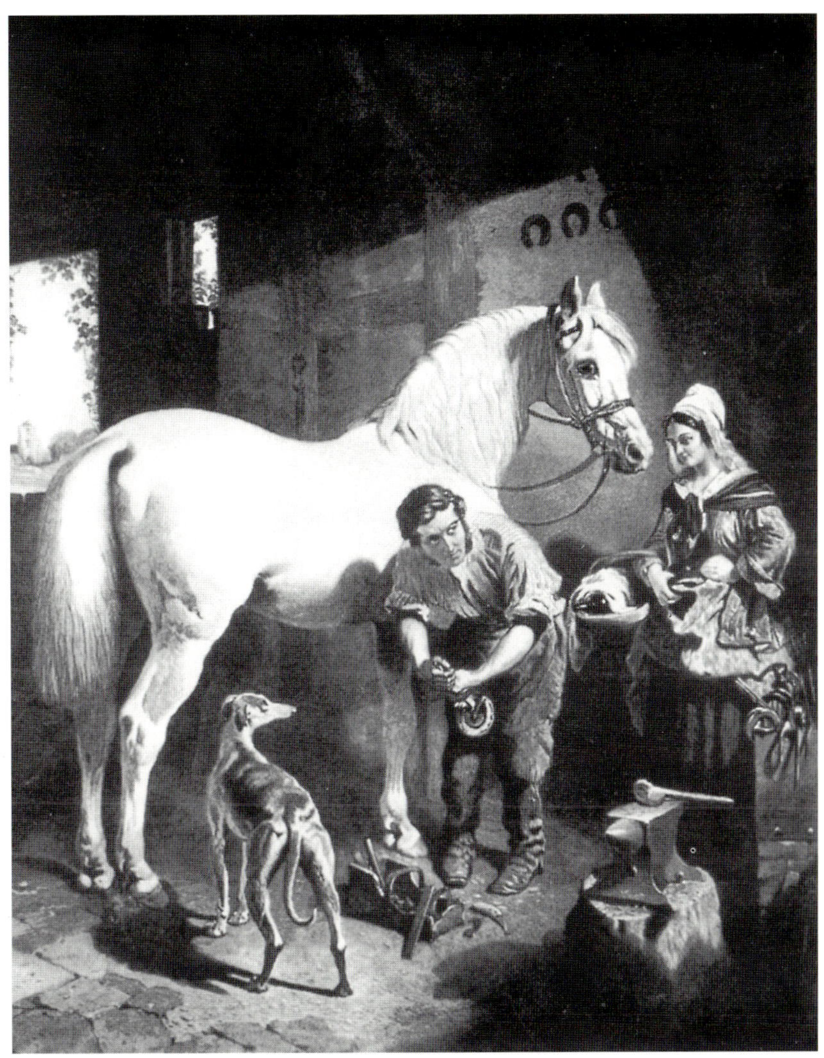

*Figure 4. Printmaker unknown,* **The Village Blacksmith.** *This is the print that hung over the bed where Lincoln died. (Harold Holzer)*

the modest Petersen House chamber grew larger and larger to accommodate the number of people that propriety-driven publishers believed must be portrayed in it, and the artist's evident desire to aggrandize the circumstances surrounding a great man's death.[19]

Currier & Ives was first, fast, and fairly accurate, but not yet satisfied. Within days the firm had second thoughts about one major omission: the new president, Andrew Johnson, was not portrayed in their original deathbed scene. They reconsidered and removed General Halleck from the second version of their print, replacing him with the man who succeeded Lincoln *(Figure 5)*. With Johnson included, a print of the last moments of President Lincoln could also become a print of the first moments of President Johnson, symbolizing peaceful succession and national continuity in the face of crisis.

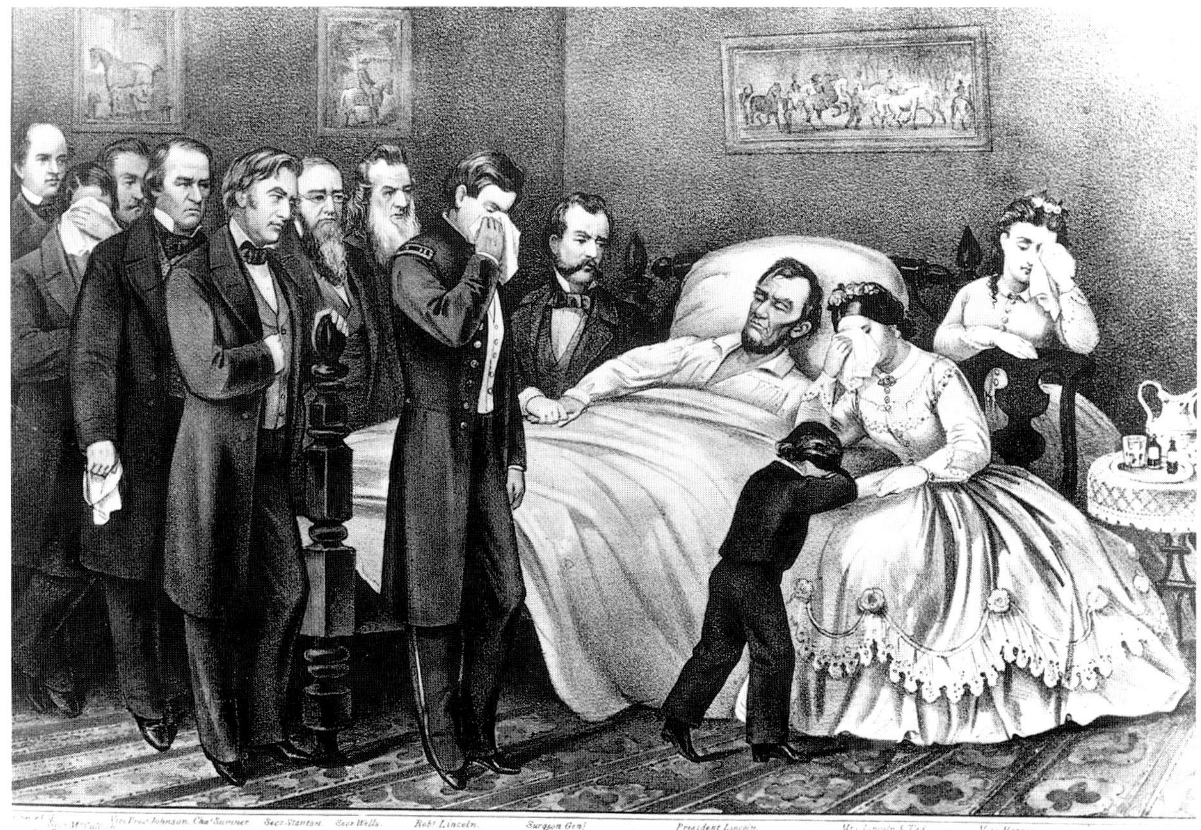


*Figure 5. Currier & Ives,* **Death of President Lincoln....** *Lithograph, New York, 1865. For the second state of their deathbed print, the lithographers substituted Vice President Andrew Johnson for General Henry W. Halleck (fourth from left). (The Lincoln Museum)*

Perhaps that is why a third and final interpretation of Lincoln's death by Currier & Ives proved the most politically correct of all three *(Figure 6)*. Here, Johnson advanced even further toward the bedside. Mary Lincoln, on the other hand, was banished to the doorway, weeping alone as her husband expires inside. To demonstrate a final farewell and reconciliation by Lincoln's political enemies, the scene also included the recently named Chief Justice of the United States, Salmon P. Chase, who in reality never visited Lincoln's bedside that fateful night.

Most printmakers preferred to keep Mary in their scenes. Currier & Ives New York neighbor, engraver H. H. Lloyd—in yet another derivative work—exercised considerable artistic latitude by placing Mary sprawled across the bed, Tad kneeling in prayer, and Edwin Stanton so squashed by fellow witnesses that he seems to find it difficult to raise his right

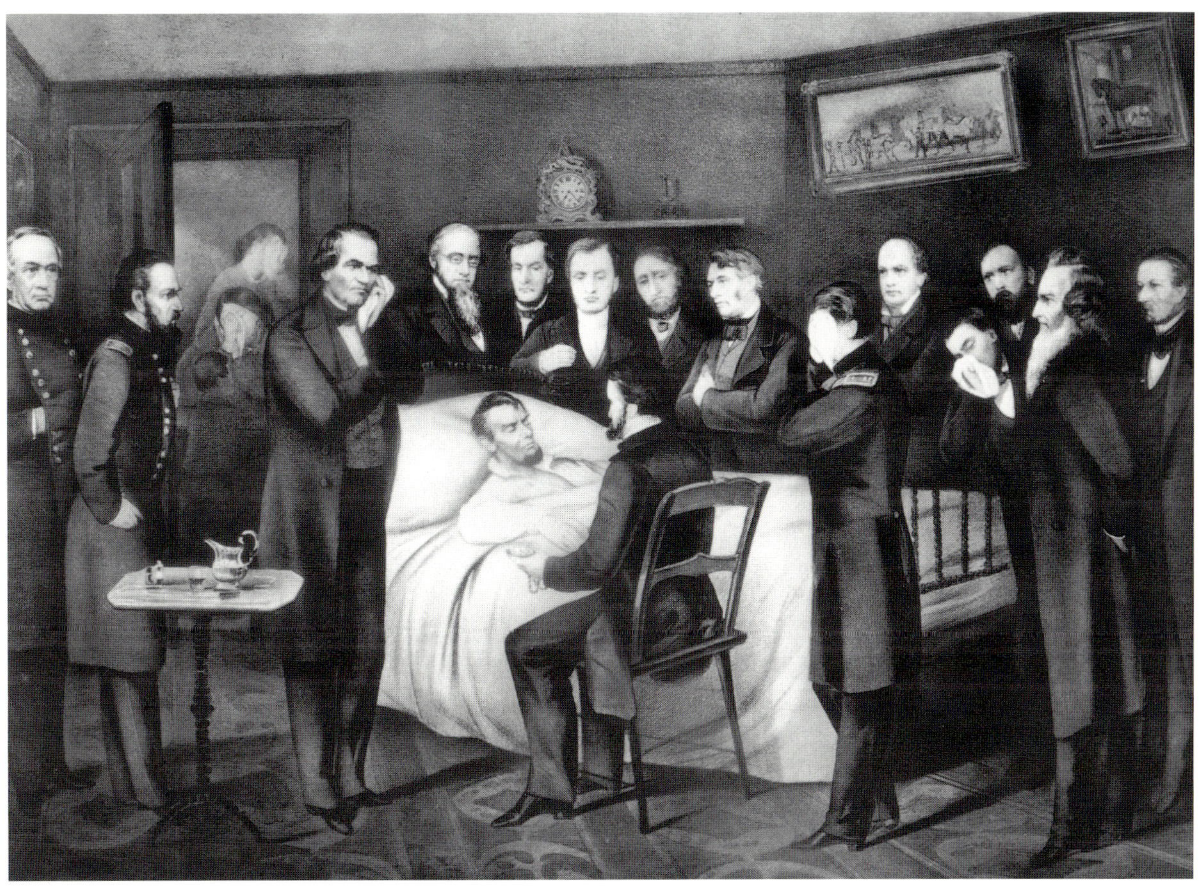

*Figure 6. Currier & Ives,* **The Death Bed of the Martyr President Abraham Lincoln Washington, Saturday Morning April 15th 1865, at 22 Minutes Past 7 O'Clock.** *Lithograph, New York, 1865. For their third interpretation of Lincoln's death scene, the printmakers placed Mary Lincoln outside the room. (Library of Congress)*

arm to wipe away a tear *(Figure 7)*. The deception—and the fantasy—were only beginning. But there were some exceptions to the rule of publish first and research later.

One "last moments" scene, for example, actually showed blood on the pillow, and the attending doctor realistically checking the dying man for a pulse. A surprisingly accurate German-made print featured a chillingly accurate spool bed much like the one in which Lincoln had died *(Figure 8)*. And another German print of the same year, by Gustave May of Frankfurt, after an original by J. H. Bufford of Boston, managed to convey the impression of the dying moment with considerable power, except perhaps for Andrew Johnson's pose of casual indifference *(Figure 9)*.

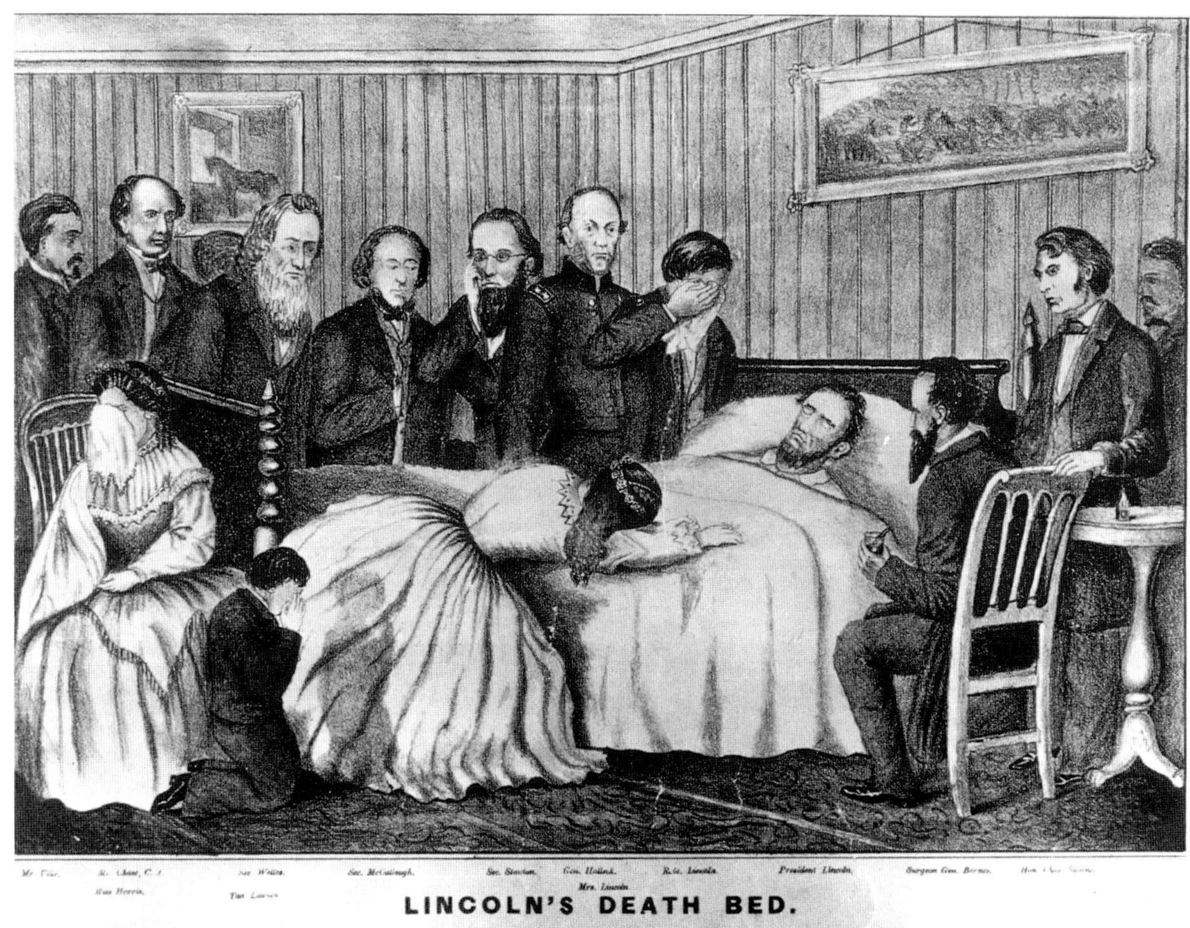


*Figure 7. H. H. Lloyd & Co.,* **Lincoln's Death Bed. 453 Tenth Street, Washington, D.C.** *Wood engraving, New York, ca. 1865. The scene showed Mary Lincoln sprawled across the bed, and Tad Lincoln—who in reality was not present—kneeling nearby. (The Lincoln Museum)*

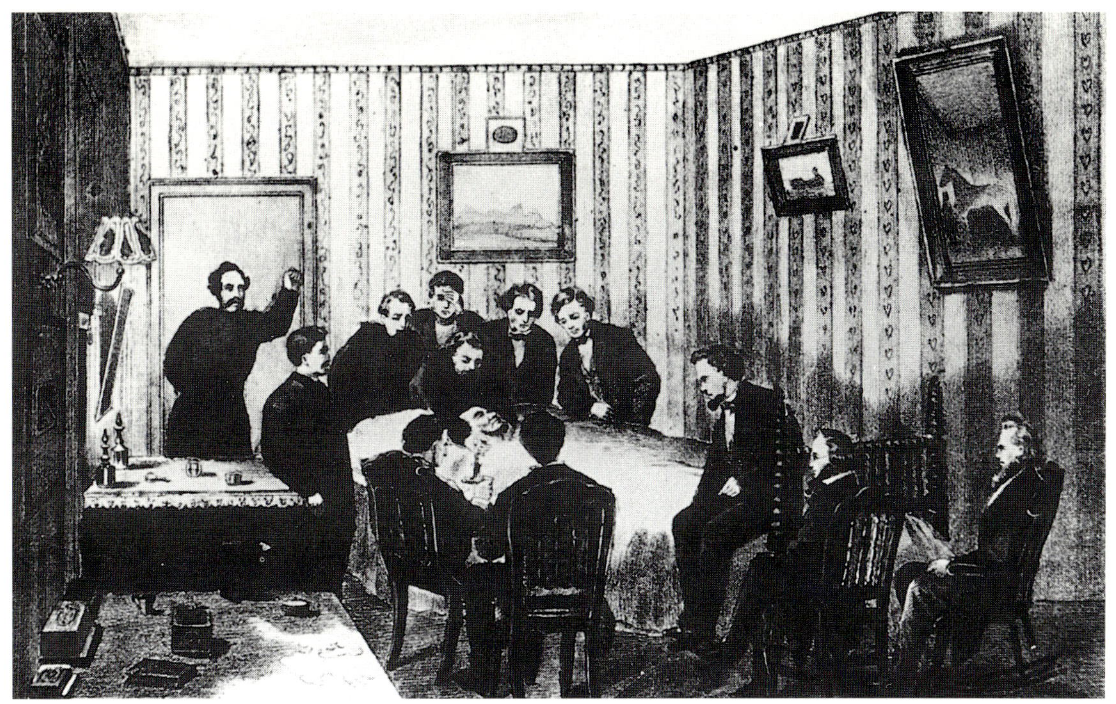

*Figure 8. Printmaker unknown,* **Lincoln's letzte Stunde. Lincoln's last hour. La dernière heure de Lincoln.** *Lithograph, Germany, ca. 1865. (Frank and Virginia Williams Collection)*

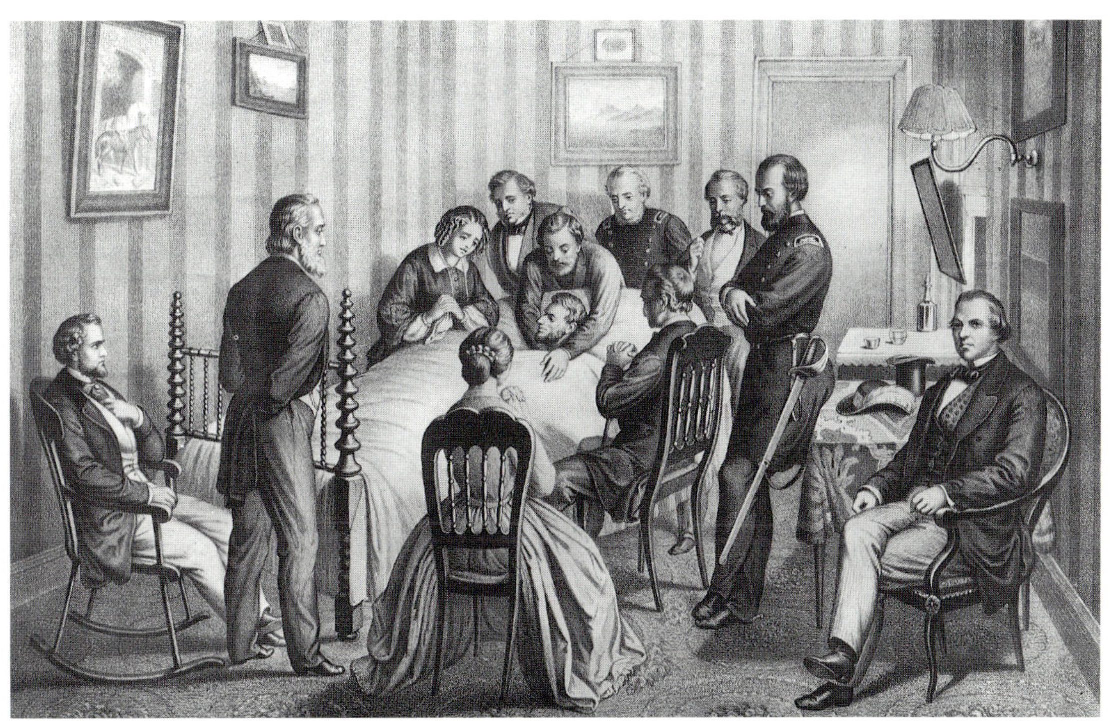

*Figure 9. Gustave May,* **Die Letzten Augenblicke des Prasidenten Lincoln. Am 15 April 1865. The Last Moments of the President Lincoln. 15 April 1865.** *Lithograph, Frankfurt, Germany, ca. 1865. A variation on the print issued by May's unknown German competitor (See Fig. 8), this print added the dispassionate Andrew Johnson at right. Both prints owed a debt to a remarkably similar death-room print by Boston lithographer J. H. Bufford. (The Lincoln Museum)*

Closer to home, lithographers E. B. & E. C. Kellogg of Hartford, Connecticut produced a print with a unique, head-on perspective. It was as original as their unique, rear-view companion assassination print—which was marred by bizarre errors like the inclusion of a Tad-sized figure depicted as "Young Petersen," as if the boarding house owner's son actually would have been allowed into President Lincoln's death chamber *(Figure 10).*

Some prints erred on the side of grandeur, like the eerily photographic engraving by C. A. Asp of Washington *(Figure 11).* But it suffered from rigidity of pose and impreciseness of background while the skill of the artist made it look perhaps too realistic for comfort. Its rarity may suggest that it was unpopular in its day.

Other prints remained helplessly shackled to the propriety of including Lincoln's successor. In J. L.

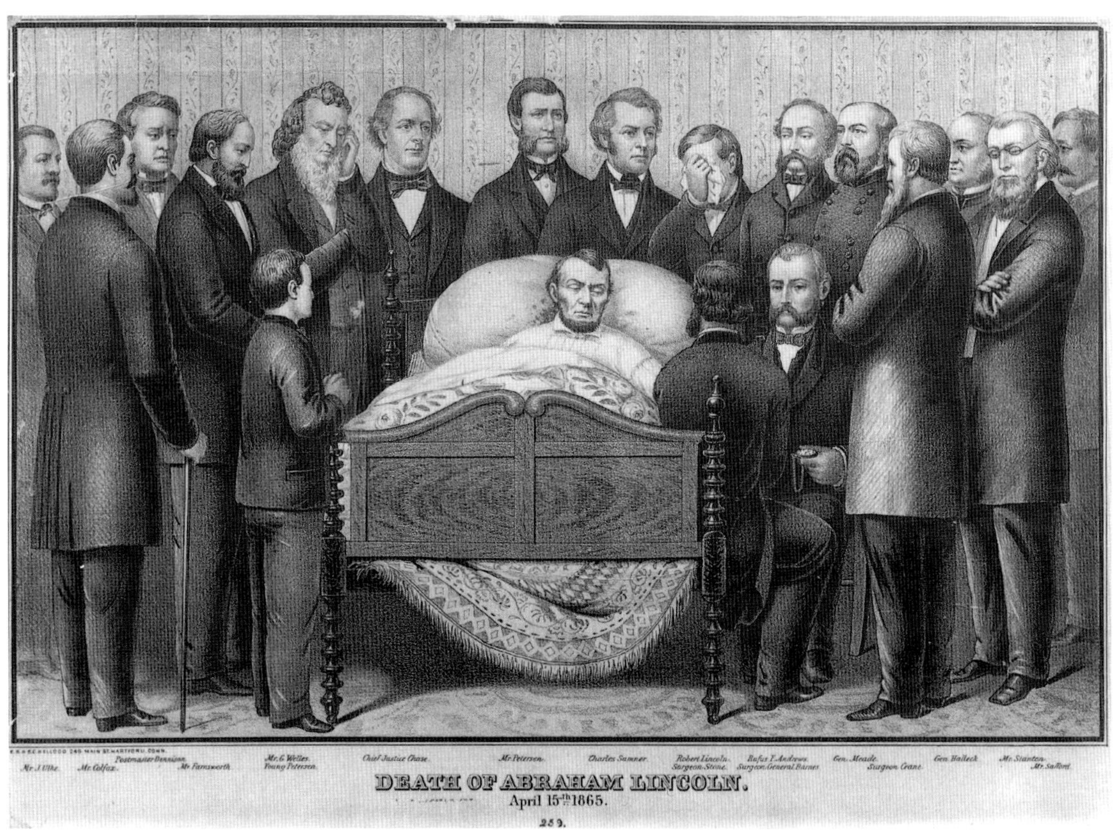


*Figure 10. E. B. & E. C. Kellogg,* **Death of Abraham Lincoln**. April 15th 1865. *Lithograph, Hartford, Connecticut, 1865. Currier & Ives' chief East Coast rivals for timely lithographs produced a death scene with a distinctive head-on perspective. (Harold Holzer)*

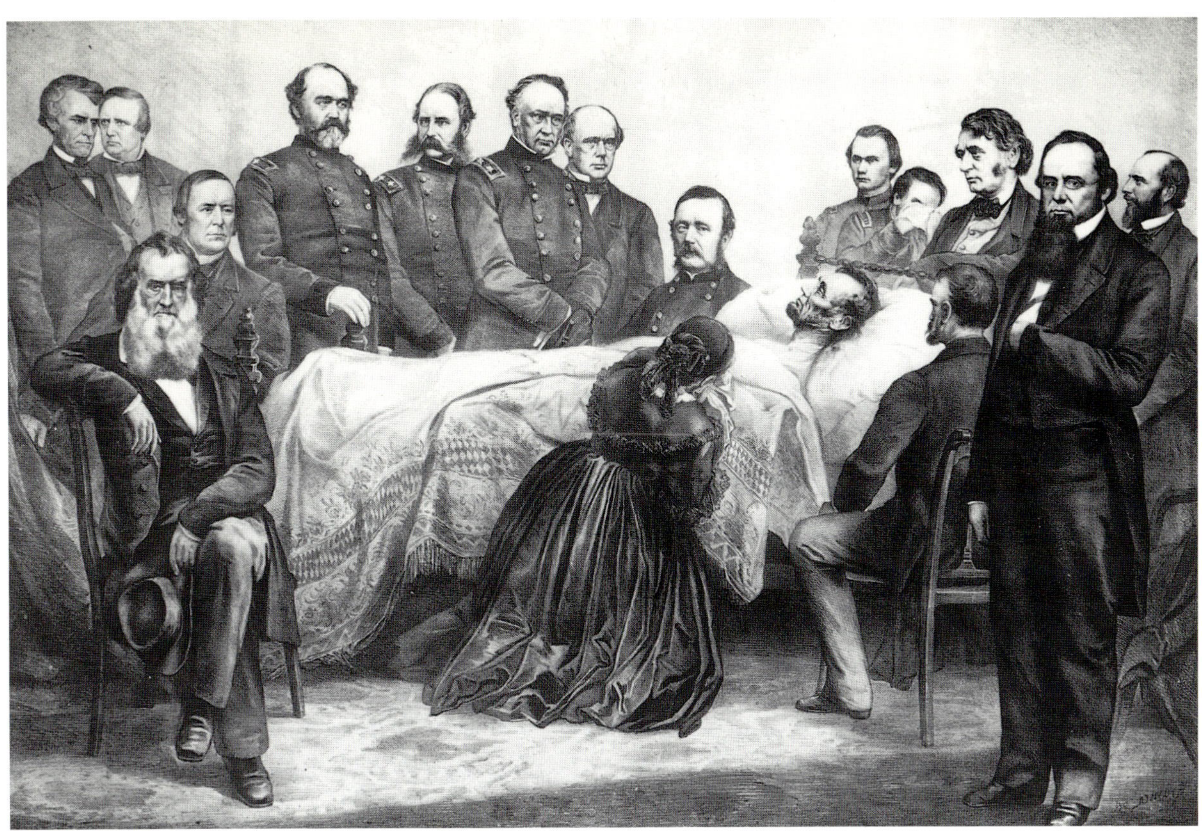

*Figure 11. C. A. Asp,* **Death Bed of Lincoln**. *Engraving, Washington, ca. 1865. This unique scene combines vivid portraiture and a complete lack of embellishment to portray the death room. It was co-published by Jones & Clark of New York and W. M. Kohl of Philadelphia. (Library of Congress)*

Magee's deathbed lithograph, Johnson even got to hold Lincoln's hand as the attending pastor delivered a final sermon *(Figure 12).* The clergyman is not the Reverend Phineas D. Gurley who was, in fact, present. Mary Lincoln, meanwhile, is relegated to the other side of the bed where she seems to be sharing an incestuous kiss with Robert. The absent Chase is included too.

The Washington photographer Alexander Gardner copyrighted his own composite scene, which did feature the Reverend Phineas D. Gurley standing at the center *(Figure 13).* Twice during the night, Gurley said prayers while visitors knelt.[20] But in Gardner's eerily realistic photo-montage, his stoic presence is not sufficiently comforting to prevent both Mary and Robert Lincoln from dissolving into tears, the latter on the shoulder of Senator Charles Sumner.

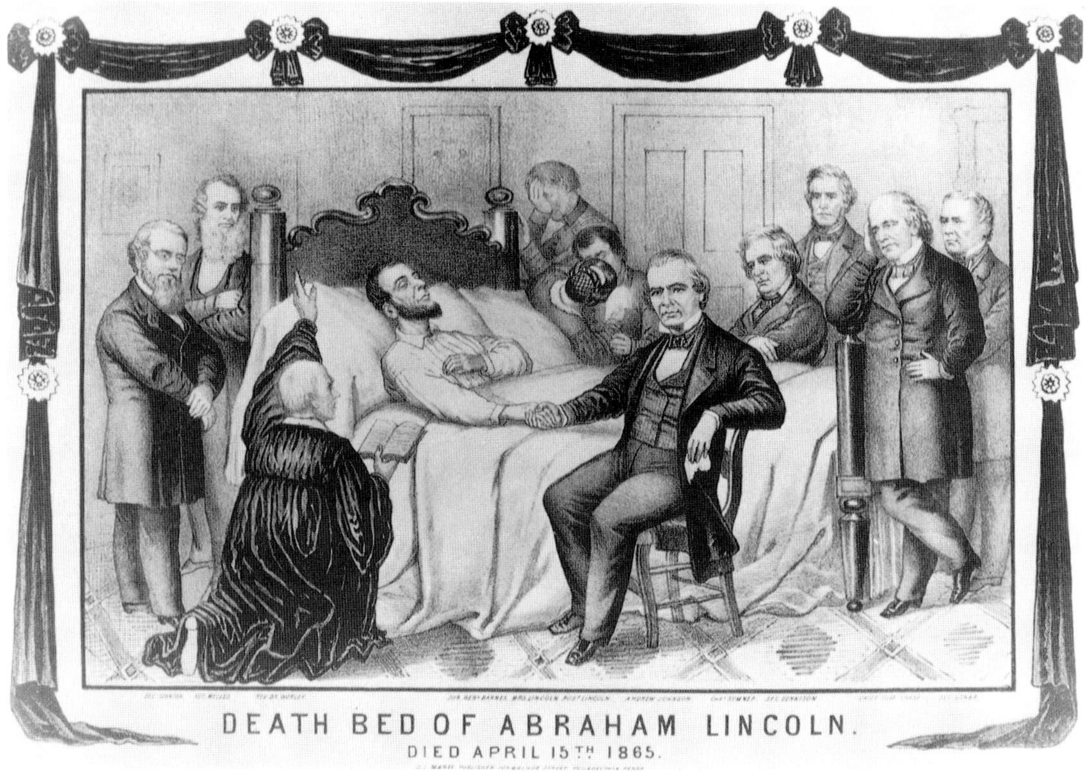


*Figure 12. J. L. Magee,* **Death Bed of Abraham Lincoln. Died April 15th 1865.** *Lithograph, Philadelphia, ca. 1865. The oddest of all deathbed prints: Andrew Johnson holds the dying Lincoln's hand while Mary appears to be kissing her son passionately in the background. The entire scene is framed as a stage set. (Frank and Virginia Williams Collection)*

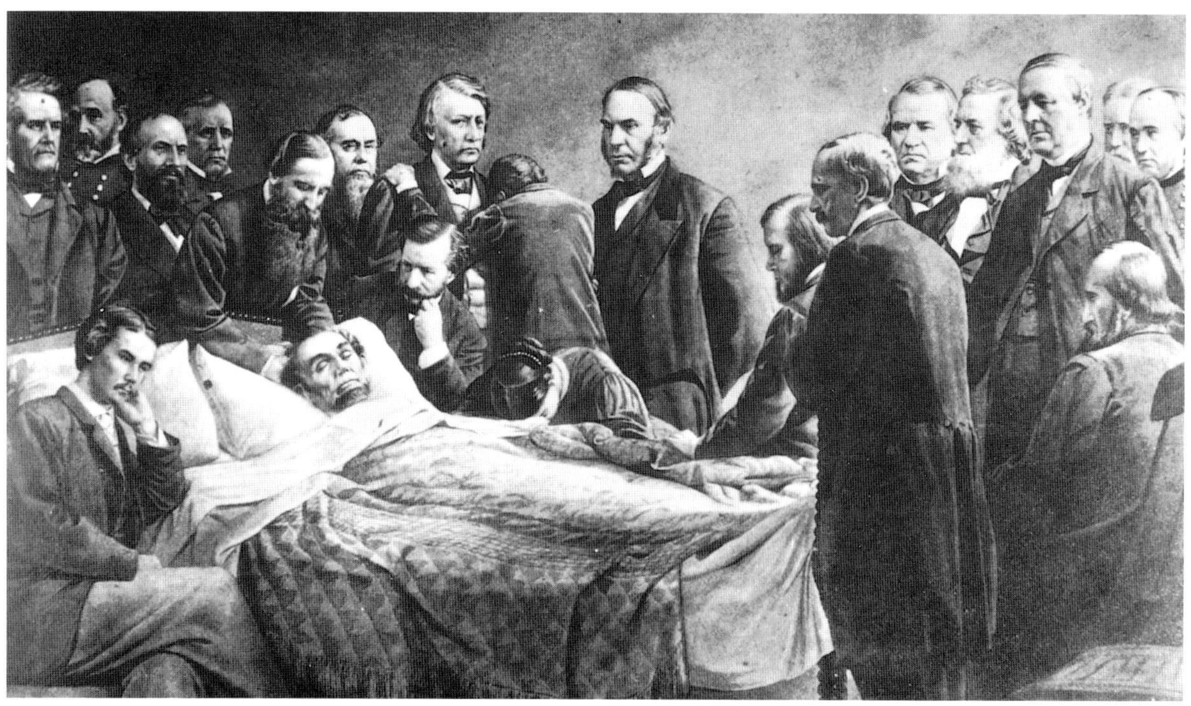

*Figure 13. Alexander Gardner,* **The Last Moments of Lincoln, 15th April, 1865.** *Painted by E. H. Miller, Published by Philip & Solomon. Photo-montage, Washington, 1866. (Library of Congress)*

Prints ranged from the ridiculous to the sublime, if fanciful. Max Rosenthal of Philadelphia produced a colorful print remarkable not so much for the portraiture of the eyewitnesses, which was good, but because of the appearance of angels come to fetch the nation's newest martyr to a heaven—seen at the top of the clouds overhead—already occupied by George Washington *(Cover, Figure 14).*

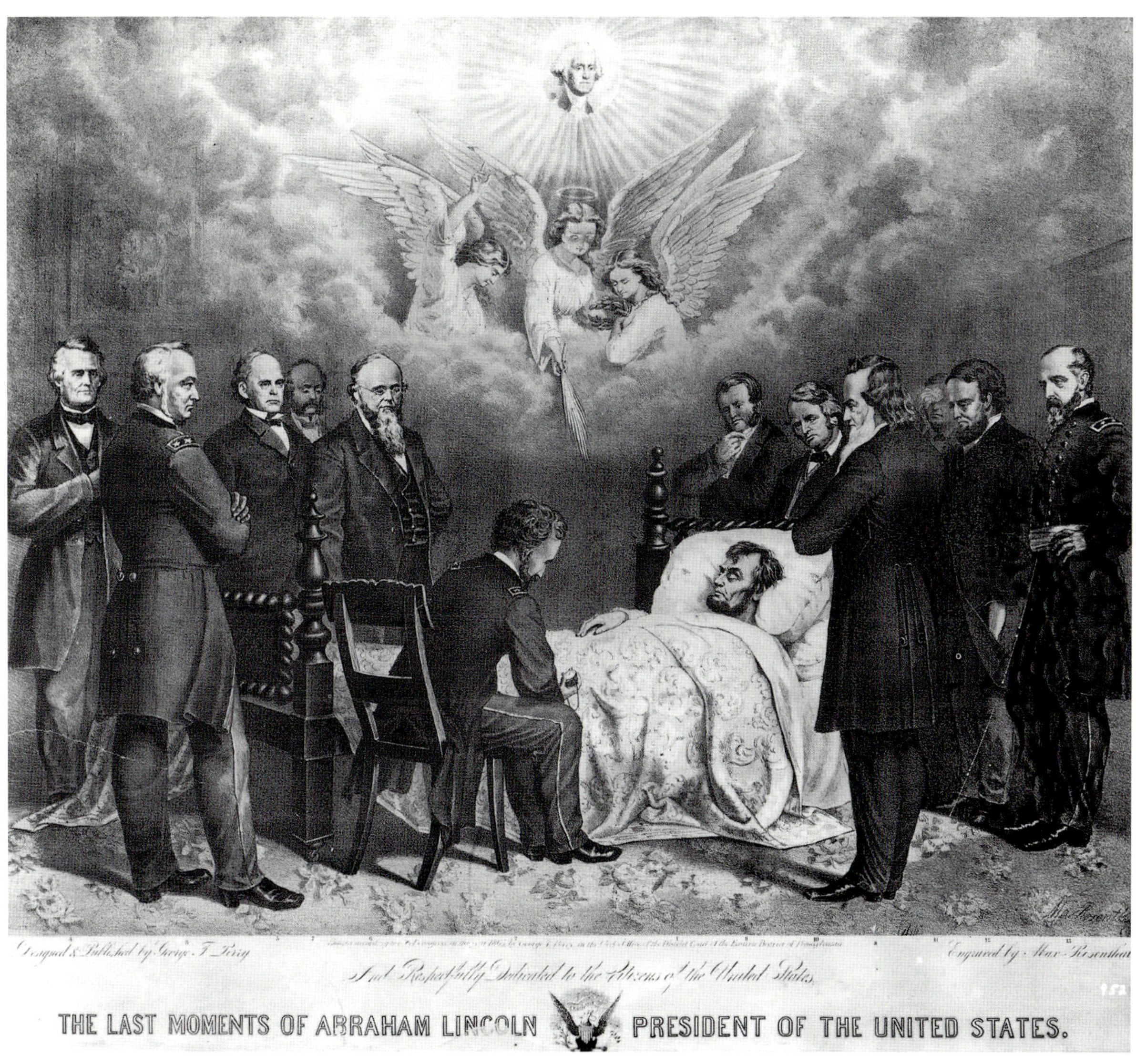


*Figure 14. Max Rosenthal,* **The Last Moments of Abraham Lincoln President of the United States, April 15th 1865.** *Designed and published by Joseph Hoover, printed by L. N. Rosenthal. Lithograph, Philadelphia, 1865. As George Washington—in the form of a stellar divinity—looks on, angels from the afterworld descend to take Abraham Lincoln to heaven. The print is a hand-colored lithograph, although artist Rosenthal took pains to credit himself as "engraver," suggesting the more expensive form of popular print, and then grandly dedicated the picture to the "people of the United States." (The Lincoln Museum)*

Perhaps the most lavish and skillfully marketed, even if not the most accurate of all the deathbed scenes, was the work of Alexander Hay Ritchie. Ritchie was the printmaker who had engraved artist Francis B. Carpenter's justly famous painting of the first reading of the Emancipation Proclamation, one of the best-selling Lincoln prints ever.

He took two years to produce a painting of *The Death of President Lincoln*, which he then engraved himself *(Figure 15)*. Although he claimed that he personally visited the Petersen House to make sketches, Ritchie's work nonetheless depicted no fewer than 26 recognizable onlookers (identified in a separately published key—in a room that in reality could not have accommodated more than six or seven of them at once *(Figure 16)*. Here the tiny death chamber took on the grand proportions of a royal chamber, and with it, Lincoln's final moments assumed the trappings of the death of a king. At the same

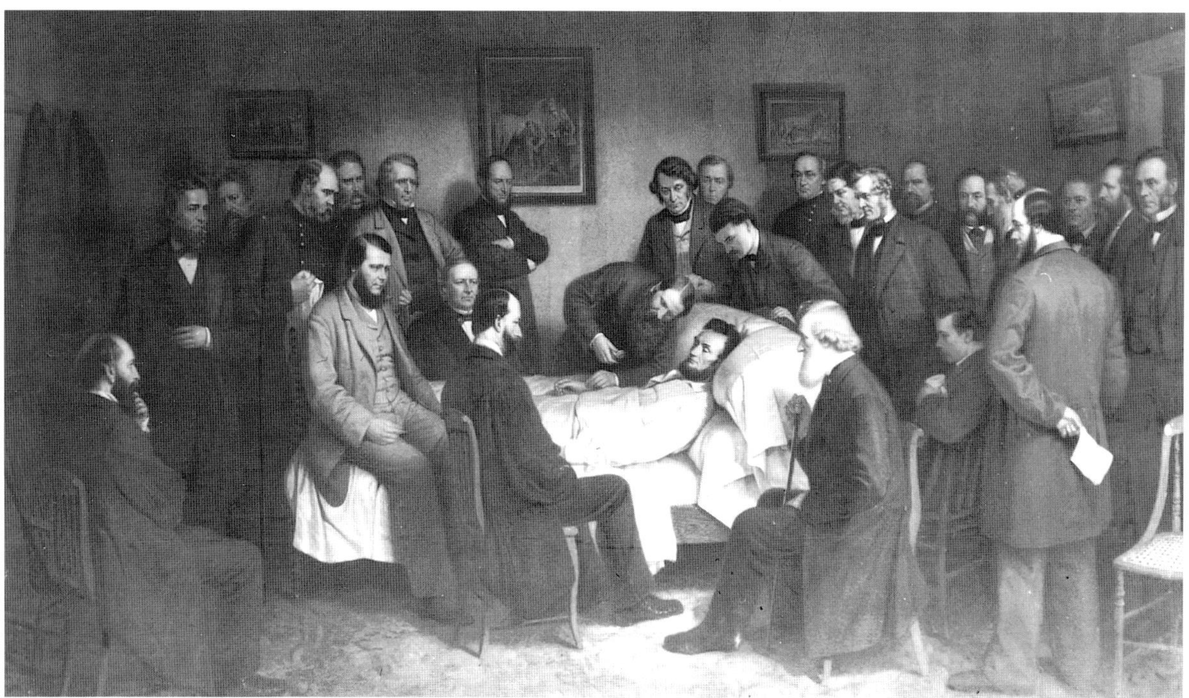

*Figure 15. A. H. Ritchie,* **Death of Lincoln.** *Engraving, New York, 1868. One of the largest, handsomest, and most lavish of all Lincoln deathbed prints, but also one of the most rigidly formal, and unrealistically crowded. (Frank and Virginia Williams Collection)*

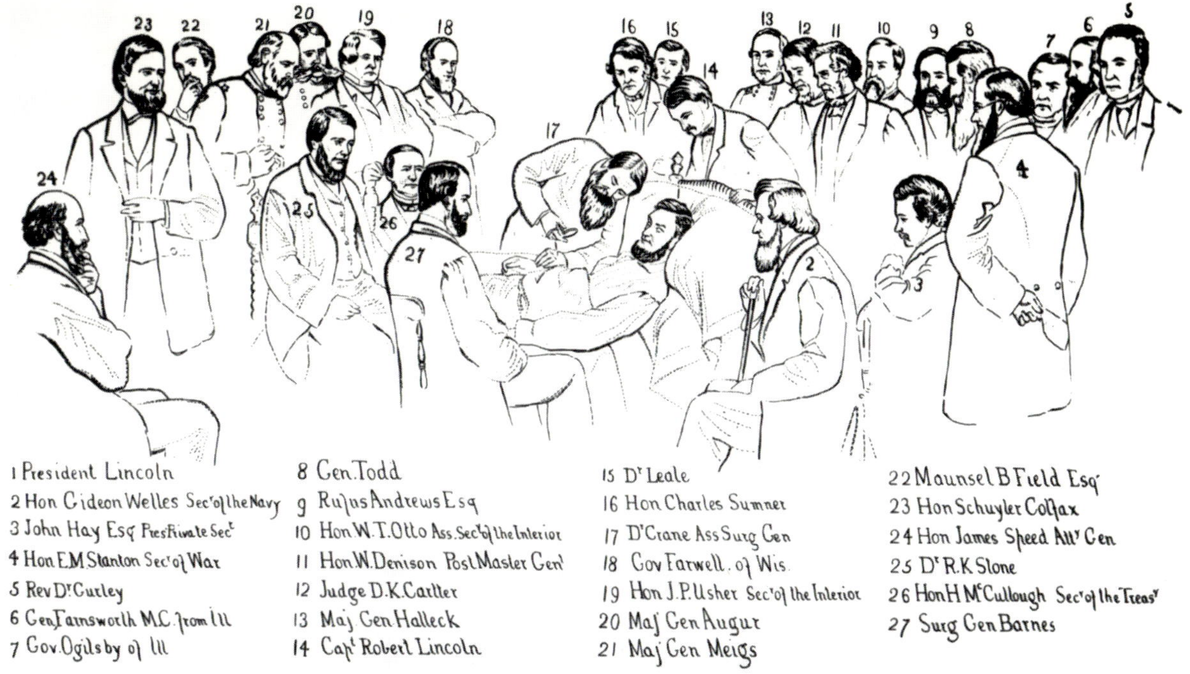


*Figure 16. This key to the Ritchie print (which bore no caption or identifying labels) was published as a fold-out guide to a marketing pamphlet for the engraving. (Harold Holzer)*

time, Ritchie was scrupulous enough to exclude both Vice President Johnson and Mrs. Lincoln.

Ritchie advertised heavily, probably because he published two years after his rivals did, an eternity where newsworthy pictures were concerned. His engraving was not only mammoth in size—nearly two feet by three feet—but also expensive: $20 for plain proofs and $30 for signed artist's proofs, a hefty sum in post-Civil War America.

Ritchie believed the result worth it. He boasted that the print offered not only portraiture of "striking character and individuality," but a priceless "record of the passing history of the nation." And the characters portrayed agreed. Reverend Phineas Gurley, for one, raved: "It renews my eye and heart with surprising vividness the scenes and impressions of that sadly memorable morning." It was, Gurley said, "a work of surpassing merit." And Quartermaster General Montgomery Meigs, another visitor to the deathbed that night, expressed his hope "that the engraving may well have a place in thousands of American homes."[21]

Judging by its rarity today, however, Meigs's hope—and Ritchie's—went unfulfilled. Perhaps its large size and even larger cost ruined its chances for success. Perhaps it simply arrived on the market too late to win the kind of following the less accurate, even the more laughable but more timely, interpretations had excited. But we know that only a few short years ago, a cache of mint-condition, signed artist's proofs was unearthed at the John Hay Library at Brown University, unseen, and apparently unsold, for more than a century.

But Ritchie, too, would be outdone in pictorial hyperbole. John H. Littlefield's vision of the death room, published in 1866, offered an even grander rendering of the scene *(Figure 17).* No fewer than 25 people were shown seated or standing around Lincoln's bedside, without any evidence that the multitude had been the least bit crowded by what in reality would have been a chokingly claustrophobic experience.

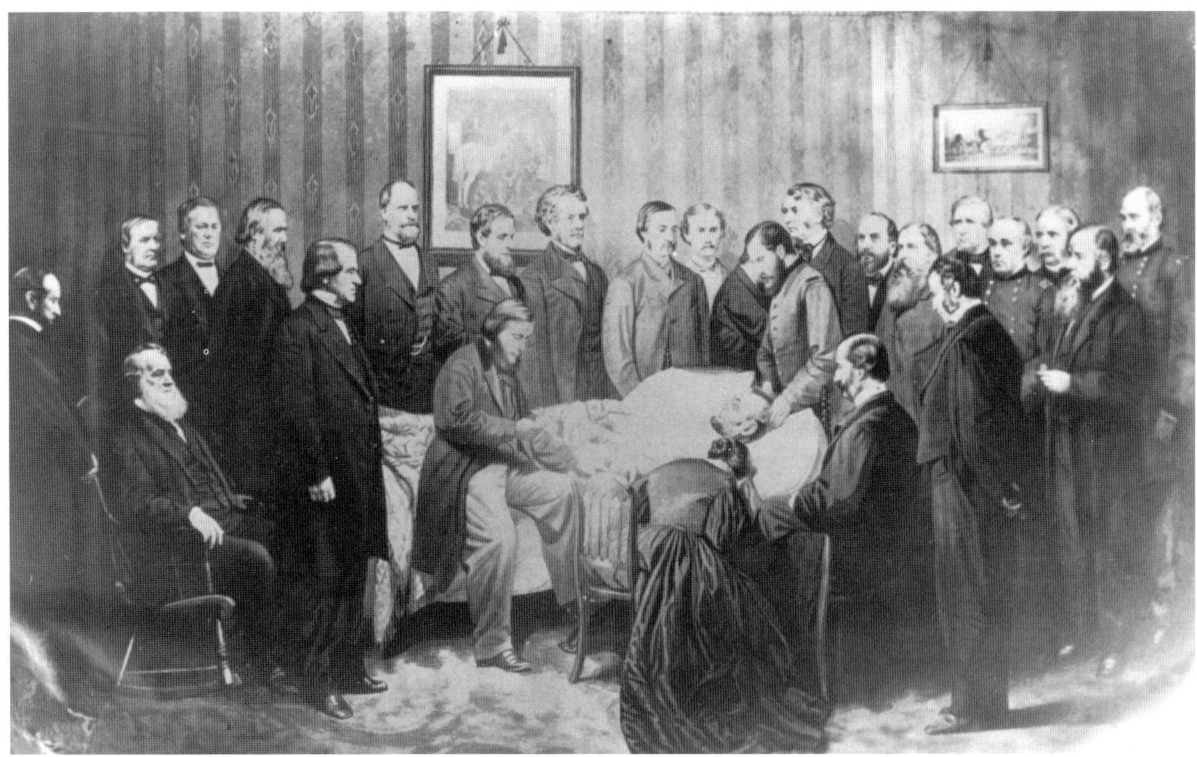

*Figure 17. John H. Littlefield,* **Death-Bed of Lincoln. April 15th 1865**. *Photographs by John Goldin. Engraving, Washington, 1866. No fewer than 24 eyewitnesses crowd the scene in this print adaptation of a period painting. (The Lincoln Museum)*

Also at Brown University is Alonzo Chappel's huge canvas, *The Death of Lincoln. (Figure 18).* This oil painting further expanded the small Petersen House room to hold a staggering 47 mourners, all of whom actually were there at one time or another during the night, but not together. By comparison, Ritchie depicted 26 and John H. Littlefield 25. Hermann Faber's contemporaneous sketch had shown 14 persons, even then, far more than the room could hold.

Widely exhibited and lavishly praised when it was completed, Chappel's work boasted perhaps the most realistic portraiture of any of the death-bed scenes ever attempted by artist or printmaker *(Figures 19, 20).* The painter achieved these life-like qualities through an ingenious and audacious shortcut: convincing the principals he intended to portray in the work to pose for photographs assuming the precise pose that Chappel desired them to strike in his canvas.

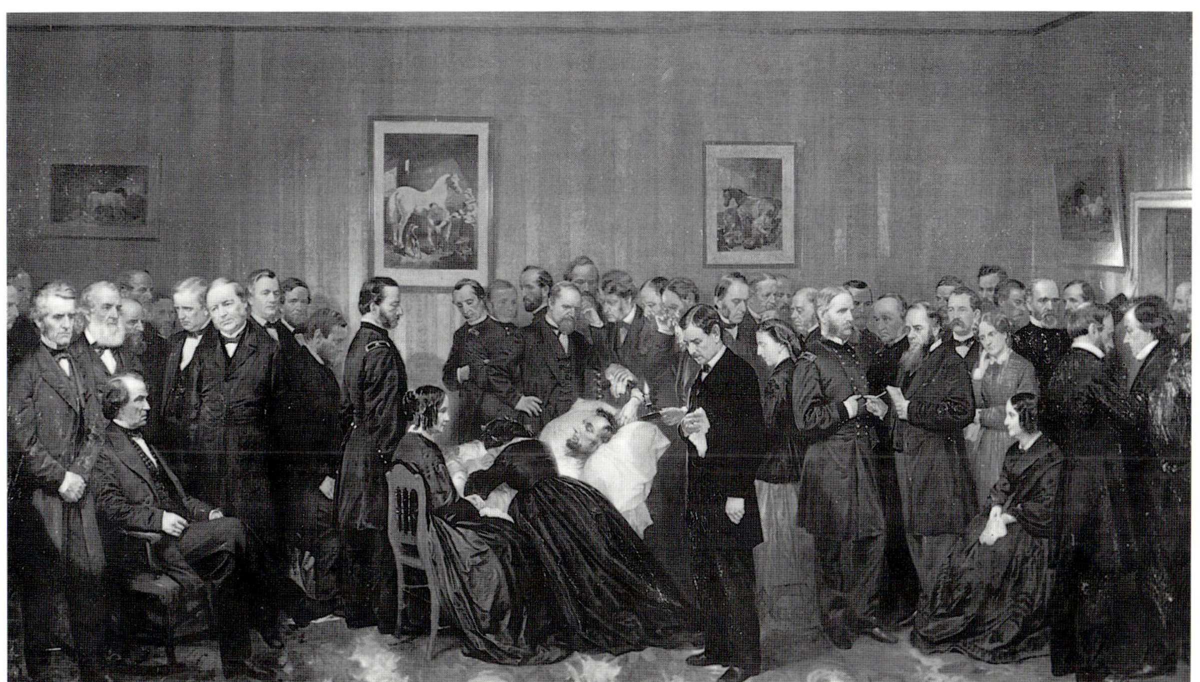

*Figure 18. Alonzo Chappel,* **The Last Hours of Lincoln**. *Oil on canvas, 52 x 89-1/2 inches, 1868, designed by John B. Bachelder. The most elaborate of all the Lincoln death scenes, Chappel's mammoth canvas was thronged by 47 figures. (Chicago Historical Society)*

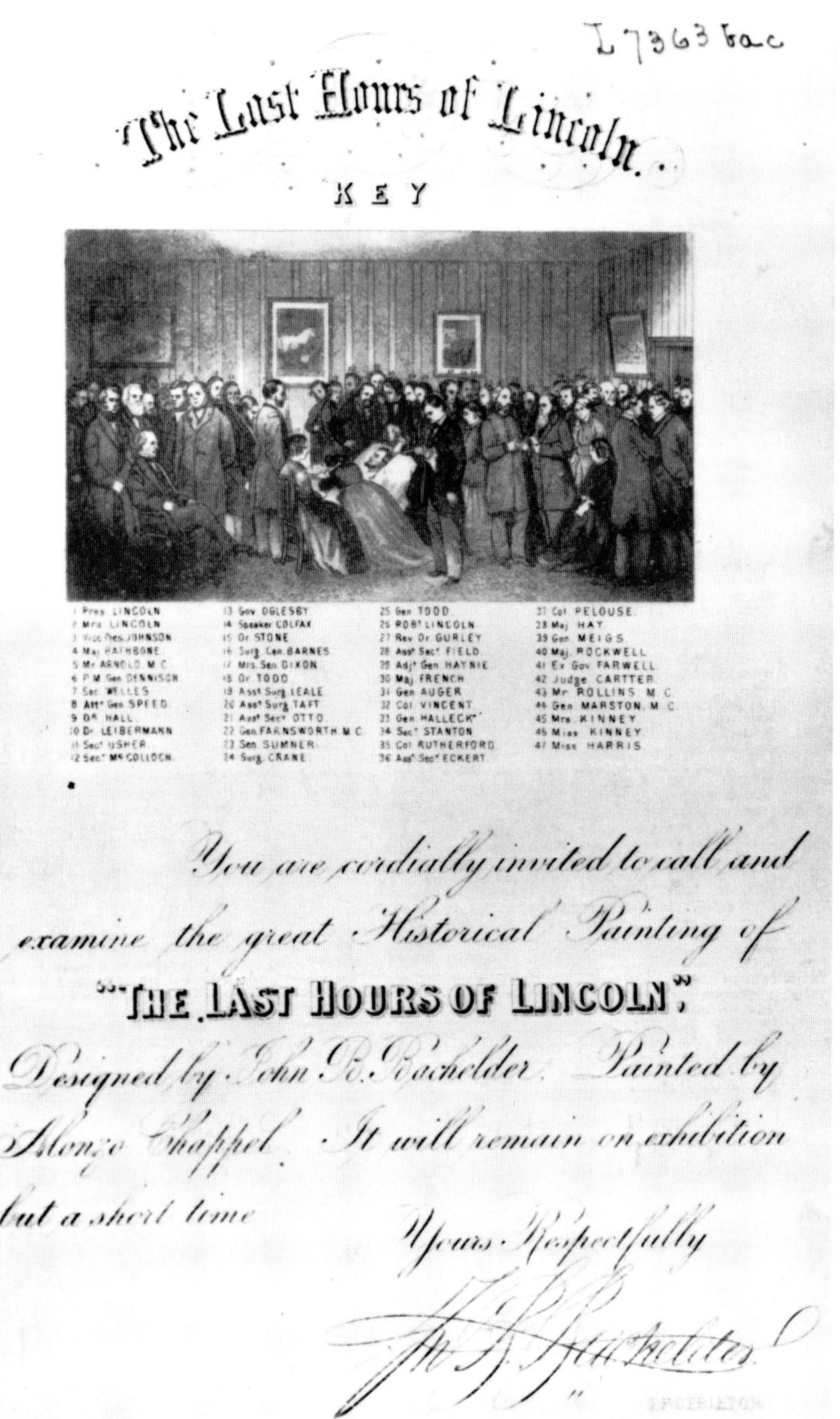



# The Last Hours of Lincoln.

KEY

1 Pres. LINCOLN
2 Mrs. LINCOLN
3 Vice Pres. JOHNSON
4 Maj RATHBONE
5 Mr ARNOLD. M.C.
6 P.M. Gen DENNISON
7 Sec. WELLES
8 Att'y Gen SPEED
9 Dr HALL
10 Dr LEIBERMANN
11 Sec'y USHER
12 Sec'y McCOLLOCH
13 Gov OGLESBY
14 Speaker COLFAX
15 Dr STONE
16 Surg. Gen BARNES
17 Mrs. Sen DIXON
18 Dr TODD
19 Asst Surg LEALE
20 Ass't Surg TAFT
21 Ass't Sec'y OTTO
22 Gen FARNSWORTH M.C.
23 Sen SUMNER
24 Surg. CRANE
25 Gen TODD
26 ROB'T LINCOLN
27 Rev Dr GURLEY
28 Ass't Sec'y FIELD
29 Adj't Gen HAYNIE
30 Maj FRENCH
31 Gen AUGER
32 Col VINCENT
33 Gen HALLECK
34 Sec'y STANTON
35 Col RUTHERFORD
36 Ass't Sec'y ECKERT
37 Col PELOUSE
38 Maj HAY
39 Gen MEIGS
40 Maj ROCKWELL
41 Ex Gov FARWELL
42 Judge CARTTER
43 Mr ROLLINS M.C.
44 Gen MARSTON M.C.
45 Mrs KINNEY
46 Miss KINNEY
47 Miss HARRIS

*You are cordially invited to call and examine the great Historical Painting of*

**"THE LAST HOURS OF LINCOLN,"**

*Designed by John B. Bachelder. Painted by Alonzo Chappel. It will remain on exhibition but a short time*

*Yours Respectfully*

PROPRIETOR

*Figure 19.* **Key to The Last Hours of Lincoln,** *part of an invitation "to call and examine the great Historical Painting" during "a short" exhibition. (Chicago Historical Society)*

# Brief Sayings of Eminent Men.

SURGEON-GENERAL'S OFFICE,
WASHINGTON CITY, *March* 20, 1867.

Col. J. B. BACHELDER,

SIR:—The picture of "The Last Hours of Lincoln," painted by Alonzo Chappel from your design, presents, with remarkable fidelity, the portraits of those in attendance at various times during the night of April 14, 1865, preserving truthfully the principal features of that most sad event.

Very respectfully yours,
J. K. BARNES, *Surgeon-General U. S. A., Brevet Major-General.*

---

It is certainly a work of great interest and merit. I have looked upon it with the liveliest satisfaction on account of its singularly graphic delineation of the actual scene as myself beheld it, and also because the likenesses of most of the distinguished persons presented by the painting seem to me to be very accurate and striking. P. D. GURLEY, *Pastor of the N. Y. Ave. Pres. Church.*

---

I cheerfully bear testimony to the accuracy of the Portraits of the persons present on that melancholy occasion, and especially that of the martyred President.

W. T. OTTO, *Assistant Secretary of the Interior.*

---

It gives me pleasure to testify to the accuracy with which you have represented the principal features of the scene in question, and to the fidelity of the portraits which you have introduced. You have been especially successful in the likeness of President Lincoln. JOHN HAY,

*Brevet Colonel, formerly A. D. C. to President Lincoln.*

---

The truthful likeness of President Lincoln, the fidelity of the portraits of those present on that most mournful night, and the excellent grouping of the figures, render this picture peculiarly valuable in an historical point of view, apart from its merits as a work of art.

C. H. CRANE, *Assistant Surgeon-General U. S. Army.*

---

Without possessing a critical capacity for judgment, I can say, in all sincerity, that the painting, as a whole, is faithful to the scene of the death-chamber on that eventful night, and impressively truthful in its portraiture. D. K. CARTTER, *Chief-Justice.*

☞ The above gentlemen visited President Lincoln during his last hours, and are represented in the painting.

---

It is admirable as a picture, and of great value for the fidelity of the portraits.

A. A. HUMPHREYS, *Major-General.*

---

DEAR SIR:—Permit me to thank you for the enjoyment of the luxury of grief afforded me in the viewing of the great picture commemorating "The Last Hours of Lincoln." It is deserving of great praise. If it has a fault, it is its high coloring. As I have personally known nearly all the forty odd persons who appear in it, I can speak with confidence of the truthfulness of the likenesses.

F. E. SPINNER, *Treasurer United States.*

---

The majority of the portraits could hardly be improved.

O. O. HOWARD, *Major-General.*

---

I know personally a large majority of the persons represented, and take pleasure in bearing my testimony to the singular fidelity of their portraits. IRA HARRIS, *United States Senator.*

## EXTRACT FROM A CRITICISM.

[*From the Washington Sunday Herald.*]

WASHINGTON, *March* 31, 1867.

A great picture has been designed of the "Last Hours of Abraham Lincoln." The designer is Mr. John B. Bachelder, the painter Alonzo Chappel. * * The value of such a picture of such a scene is enormous, and of a kind to ever increase with time. * * Looking like himself, from his finger-nails to his hard, protruding lip, Stanton, with paper and pencil in hand, and uplifted forefinger, is giving instructions to the soldierly General Auger, the then Military Commander of the District. * * Portraits so minutely like I have never seen, even from the brush of Elliot. * * *

The grandeur in the face of Lincoln, is grand indeed. The cold hues of death are warmed to the eye by the red rays of a candle held over him, and the flickering flare causing a Rembrandt-like effect, is very felicitously managed. The eye rests in love and pity on it, turning from those around impatiently. * * *

McCulloch who turns from the scene, and Johnson who sits in the left foreground, are wonderfully like. As is the erect Dennison beyond them; and Meigs, with his hand resting on the door-post, where he stood to prevent disturbing entrances; Dr. Stone and Surgeon-General Barnes, General Todd, Judge Otto, Sumner, Farnsworth, Speaker Colfax, and Governor Oglesby, are looking down on the face of Lincoln with an expression of respectful concern. * * * Judge Cartter and Ex-Governor Farwell stand in front of Meigs, forming the right foreground of the picture; they are given in profile and seem conversing.

The greatness of the picture lies in its correct transcription of an actual scene and perfect portraiture of American men. It is just such a work as, above all others, should be American property, for if ever there was a *National* picture, this is one. ARC.

*Figure 20. "Brief Sayings of Eminent Men," issued in praise of the Chappel painting, came from, among others, the surgeon-general who attended Lincoln and the clergyman who prayed at his deathbed. (Chicago Historical Society)*

Notwithstanding Robert Lincoln's notorious penchant for privacy, he allowed himself to be convinced to pose for one such photograph, head bowed, and clutching a handkerchief, as if in tears! It is difficult to imagine Robert tolerating such an invasion of his period of mourning, but he consented nonetheless—as did President Johnson (although Chappel ultimately chose to pose him somewhat differently in the painting), and Lincoln Administration cabinet officers Hugh McCulloch and Edwin Stanton *(Figure 21).* The final painting, designed by Jonathan Batchelder, famous for his exhaustively researched Gettysburg print panoramas, was no less complex than one of his battle scenes.

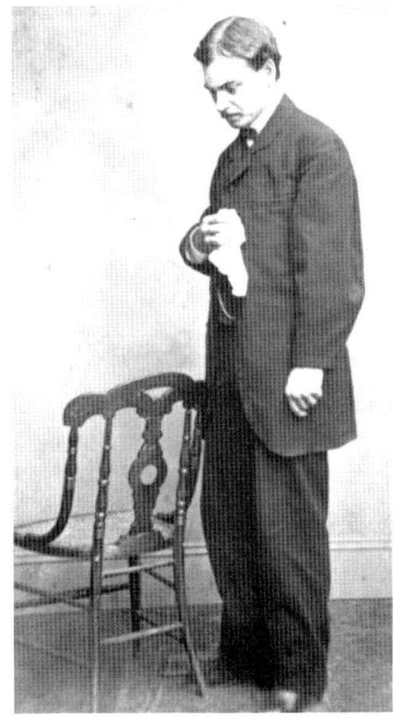

*Figure 21. The dead president's son, Robert T. Lincoln (left), Vice President Andrew Johnson (bottom, left), Secretary of the Treasury Hugh McCulloch (bottom, center), and Secretary of War Edwin M. Stanton (bottom, right) pose for photographs commissioned by designer John B. Bachelder and painter Alonzo Chappel for* **The Last Hours of Lincoln**. *The pictures were probably taken around 1868 at the Brady Gallery in Washington. Robert Lincoln, McCulloch, and Stanton were ultimately painted in these precise poses; Johnson was depicted in the final canvas seated. (Chicago Historical Society)*

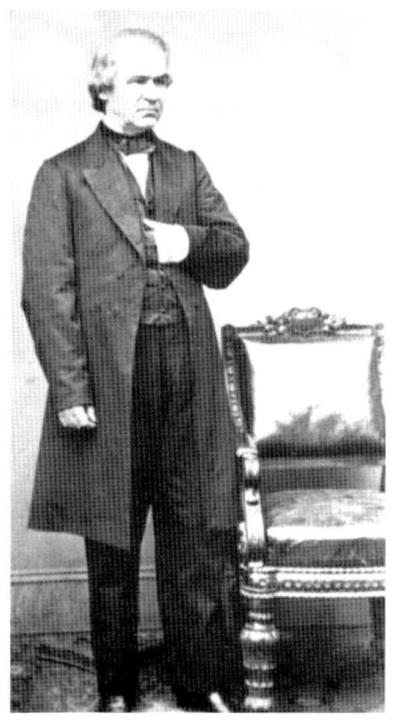

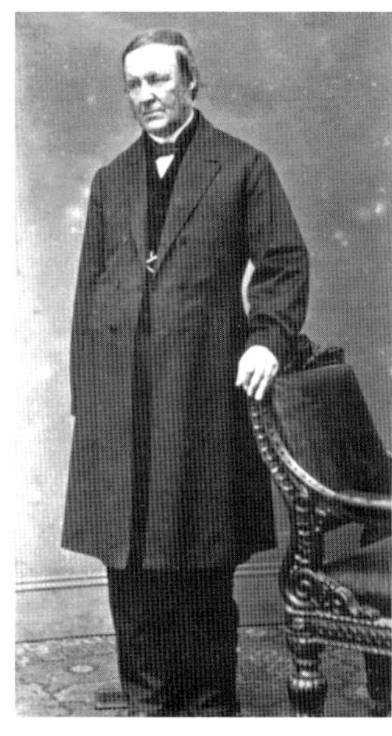

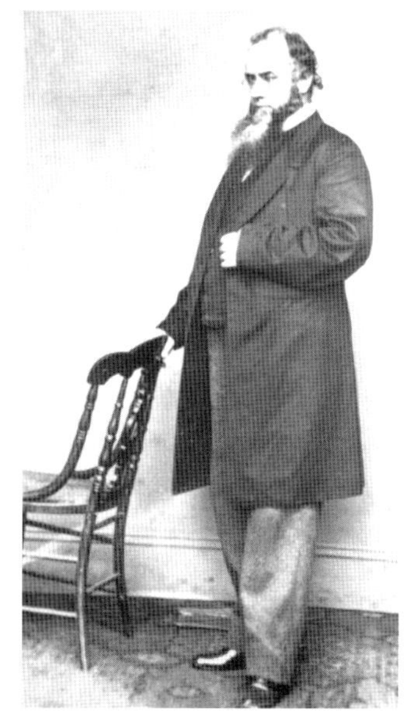

Evidently, Chappel hoped his painting would be adapted immediately as a popular print. He distributed an order book to subscribers soon after the painting was unveiled, promising that "a First Class, Steel Engraving, from this beautiful painting is about to be published," at 31 x 17 inches in size. Artists' proofs were offered at $100, India proofs at $60, plain proofs at $35, and plain prints at $15—healthy prices indeed for the 1860s.

And the surviving original subscription book, now in the Chicago Historical Society, reveals no shortage of customers *(Figure 22).* Robert Lincoln and Ulysses S. Grant each ordered the most expensive proof available.

Yet there is no evidence that a print of the Chappel painting ever made it to the marketplace in the 19th century. The only known print adaptation,

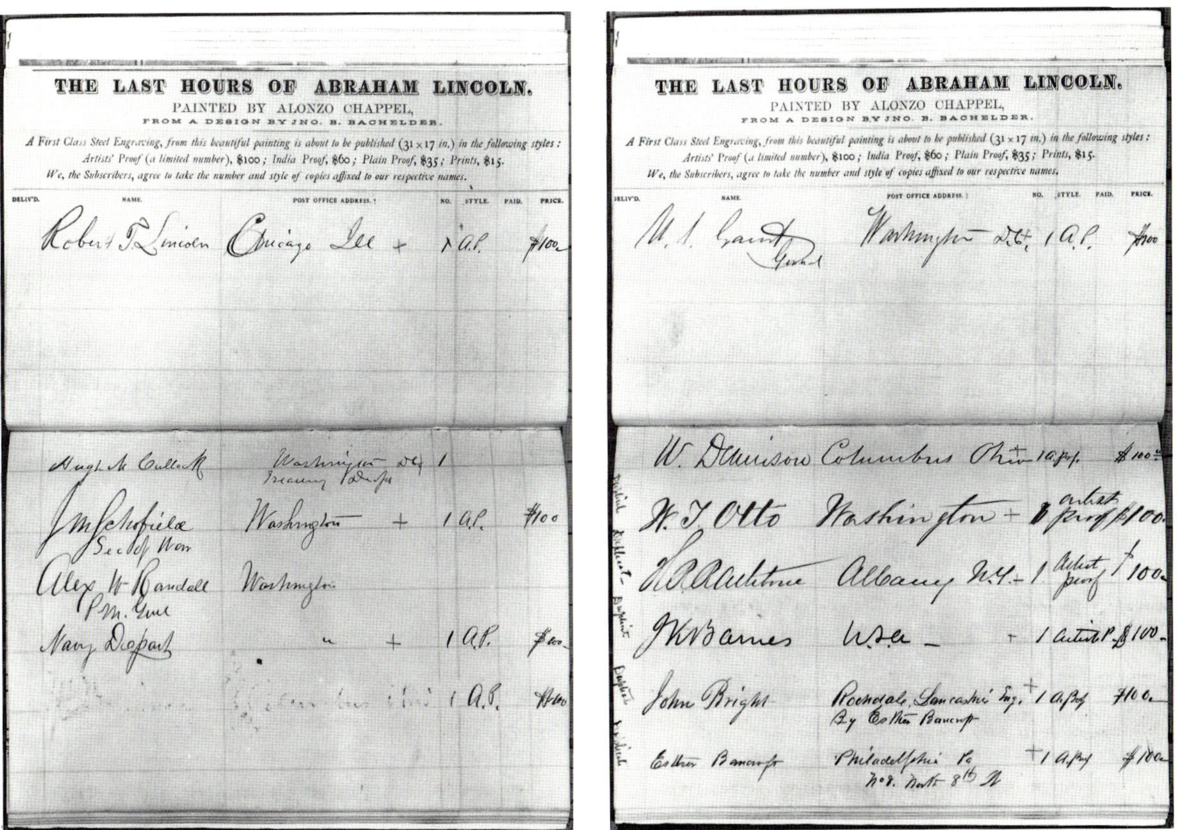

THE LAST HOURS OF ABRAHAM LINCOLN.

PAINTED BY ALONZO CHAPPEL,

FROM A DESIGN BY JNO. B. BACHELDER.

*A First Class Steel Engraving, from this beautiful painting is about to be published (31 x 17 in.) in the following styles: Artists' Proof (a limited number), $100; India Proof, $60; Plain Proof, $35; Prints, $15.*

*We, the Subscribers, agree to take the number and style of copies affixed to our respective names.*

| DELIV'D. | NAME. | POST OFFICE ADDRESS. | NO. | STYLE. | PAID. | PRICE. |
|---|---|---|---|---|---|---|

THE LAST HOURS OF ABRAHAM LINCOLN.

PAINTED BY ALONZO CHAPPEL,

FROM A DESIGN BY JNO. B. BACHELDER.

*A First Class Steel Engraving, from this beautiful painting is about to be published (31 x 17 in.) in the following styles: Artists' Proof (a limited number), $100; India Proof, $60; Plain Proof, $35; Prints, $15.*

*We, the Subscribers, agree to take the number and style of copies affixed to our respective names.*

DELIV'D. NAME. POST OFFICE ADDRESS. NO. STYLE. PAID. PRICE.

*Figure 22. Two pages from the subscription-order book for the promised print of Chappel's* **The Last Hours of Abraham Lincoln**. *Robert Lincoln has signed on for a $100 artists' proof, as have Secretary of War John M. Schofield, Postmaster General A. W. Randall, Ulysses S. Grant, William Dennison, the Postmaster General in the Lincoln administration, and the English statesman John Bright. (Original in the Chicago Historical Society)*

a rather clumsy lithograph by one M. David of New York, did not appear until the eve of Lincoln's centennial birthday, in 1908 *(Figure 23).* By that time, Lincoln was better remembered for his simple origins than for the kind of grandiose, embellished death that Chappel had invented for him.

Like no other artist before him, Alonzo Chappel had stretched the "rubber room" into unrecognizable dimensions. He clearly believed in his project, and planned aggressively to market it. But the public simply was not buying.

KEY TO THE LAST DAY OF LINCOLN, by A. CHAPPEL; 1865.
PUBLISHED by M. DAVID; NEW YORK, 1908.

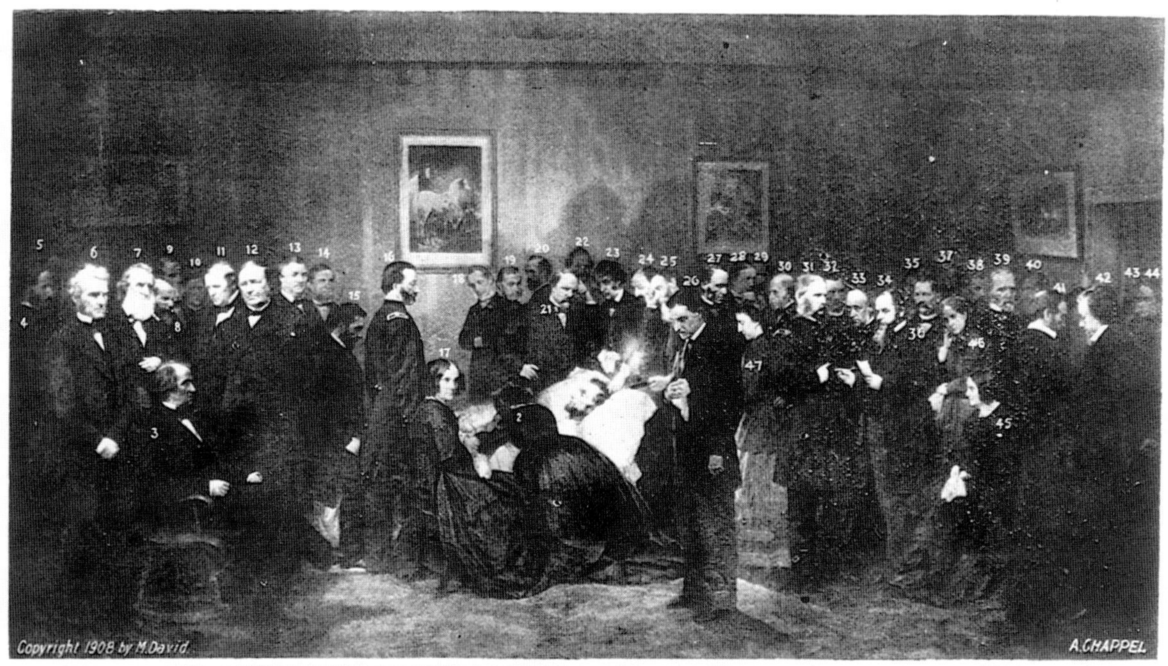


1. Pres. Lincoln
2. Mrs. Lincoln
3. Vice-Pres. Johnson
4. Maj. Rathbone
5. Mr. Arnold, P. M.
6. P. M. Gen. Dennison
7. Sec'y Welles
8. Atty. General Speed
9. Dr. Hall
10. Dr. Liebermann
11. Sec'y Usher
12. Sec'y McCulloch
13. Gov. Oglesby
14. Speaker Colfax
15. Dr. Stone
16. Surg. Gen. Barnes
17 Mrs. Sen. Dixon
18. Dr. Todd
19. Ass. Surg. Leale
20. Ass. Surg. Taft
21. Ass. Sec'y. Otto
22. Gen. Farnsworth, M. C.
23. Sen. Sumner
24. Surg. Crane
25. Gen. Todd
26. Robt. Lincoln
27. Rev. Dr. Gurly
28. Ass. Sec'y, Field
29. Adj. Gen. Haynie
30. Maj. French
31. Gen. Auger
32. Col. Vincent
33. Gen. Halleck
34. Sec'y Stanton
35. Col. Rutherford
36. Ass. Sec'y Eckert
37. Col. Pelouse
38. Maj. Hay
39. Gen. Meigs
40. Maj. Rockwell
41. Ex-Gov. Farwell
42. Judge Carter
43. Mr. Rollins, M. C.
44. Gen. Marston M. C.
45. Mrs. Kinney
46. Miss Kinney
47. Miss Harris

*Figure 23. M. David,* **Key to the Last Day of Lincoln,** *by A. Chappel. Lithograph, 1908. Testimony of the enduring popularity of the grandiose, royal-chamber view of the "rubber room," this print tribute to the Chappel painting was issued 43 years after the assassination—and just a year before the centennial of Lincoln's birth. (The Lincoln Museum)*

# CONCLUSIONS

The April 29, 1865 issue of *Harper's Weekly* had been the first to feature advertisements for pictorial products inspired by the assassination. For the next 12 weeks, its pages were filled with offerings for medals, mourning badges, and, of course, prints. By July 22, the ads had ceased. After only three months, the vogue for assassination, deathbed, and funeral prints had not only quickly come but, by the standards of 1865, had even more quickly gone.[22] Politicians kept aglow the flame of presidential martyrdom far longer than printmakers. But by the time retrospective painters like Ritchie and Chappel had produced their heroic, grandiose canvases, public interest in such depictions had faded.

Within hours, Republican members of Congress saw Lincoln's death as "a godsend" to their partisanship, expecting President Johnson to punish Southerners.[23] Stunned by the magnitude of public grief over the assassination of the president who in life had been an easy target for criticism, members of Congress chose to capitalize on a changing national mood. The following February saw a joint session of Congress commemorating the

Emancipator's birth. Historian George Bancroft offered praise, extolling Lincoln as a leader who was molded by events rather than one who shapes the times in accordance with his own will.[24]

In an irony that America's sixteenth president would have thoroughly appreciated if he himself could have choreographed a dramatic finale to his presidency, Edwin Stanton, the one-time lawyer who had pointedly dismissed Lincoln as backward in an Illinois courtroom, but later served Lincoln as Secretary of War, delivered the final benediction "in the rubber room."

"Now," Stanton said simply, "he belongs to the ages."[25]

Stanton's eloquent summation suggests that fate, in the end, allowed Lincoln to define both his life and his death. Stanton's echo from the "rubber room" helped to inspire subsequent generations to come to terms with Lincoln's leadership, just as popular art had created a secular, political heaven—however fanciful—worthy of the American saint.

# AFTERWORD

## *Restoration of the Petersen House Where Lincoln Died*

by Gary Scott
*Chief Historian, National Capital Region, National Park Service*

The Petersen House where Lincoln died, at 516 10th Street, NW (then numbered 453) in Washington, D. C., is the oldest historic house museum owned by the Federal government. It was purchased by Congress in 1896 from Lincoln collector Osborn H. Oldroyd, who had operated it for several years as a private Lincoln museum. A sad history preceded the Federal purchase.

The house holds haunting memories of Mrs. Lincoln sobbing hysterically in the front parlor while her wounded husband grappled with death in a small back bedroom, his wounded body placed diagonally in a borrowed bed too short for his lanky frame. In the back parlor, Secretary of War Edwin M. Stanton assumed dictatorial powers, interviewed witnesses, and held cabinet meetings until 7:22 a.m. the next morning when President Lincoln finally expired in the cramped, small room filled with dignitaries. Curiosity seekers stripped the room afterwards cutting up the carpet, curtains, and blood-stained sheets.

German tailor William Petersen and his wife later tried to resume a normal life, but the boarders moved away after tourists daily knocked at his door to see the room where the president died. In 1871, Petersen died of an overdose of laudanum on the front lawn of the

Smithsonian Institution. After the death of his wife four months later, a collector bought at auction the furniture from the Lincoln death room and donated the bed, chest, and chairs to the Chicago Historical Society, where they remain today.

In 1895 collector Osborn Oldroyd moved his own Lincoln collection here from Springfield, Illinois, creating Oldroyd's Lincoln Museum in the Petersen House. When Congress authorized purchase of the house in 1896, Oldroyd remained as curator. The government purchased the Oldroyd Lincoln collection in 1926.

In 1933, the house was transferred to the National Park Service. The Oldroyd Lincoln collection was moved to the Ford's Theatre Museum. Attempts were then made to restore the Petersen House with the help of the Daughters of the Union Veterans of the Civil War, who furnished the hallway. Since contemporary newspapers reported drab wallpaper in the death room, the house was refurnished with colorless wallpaper and stuffed horsehair furniture, giving the visitor a very dreary experience of a very sad event. The horsehair parlor suite had actually been brought by Oldroyd from the Lincoln home in Springfield, Illinois.

In 1959 the house was again restored as part of the National Park Service "Mission 66" program. The facade of the house was sandblasted and green, painted wood shutters were reinstated for the first time in decades. The stone front stoop with its quaint iron railings was rebuilt. In the rear a first floor later addition adjacent to the alley was removed. A new stairway now led visitors out the second story back porch to the basement hallway and then out the front basement door. Wallpaper created from a fragment found in the Smithsonian Institution was hung in the Lincoln death room.

Then in 1965, *American Heritage Magazine* published a newly discovered original photograph of the death room taken the day after Lincoln's death by photographer and boarder Julius Ulke. It showed a different pattern of striped wallpaper in the death room.

In 1978 water seepage, through plaster and wallpaper, dictated yet another restoration. A decade earlier Ford's Theatre had been lavishly restored, while the Petersen House grew shabby. As an NPS historian, I was placed in charge of the restoration, which continued for two years until 1980. Workers stripped the walls down to the original plaster, then patched holes and sagging plaster with new plaster on extended wire lathe. Much original plaster remains.

Upon stripping the paint around the front door and facade windows, we found many layers of Victorian green paint under the top white layers. The third layer of green was selected as the appropriate 1865 layer of paint. Following an 1880s photo we painted the shutters and window trim the same shade of our third layer of green and stained the front door a dark wood color.

The evidence for the recreation of the room where Lincoln died included two contemporary pictorial newspaper wood engravings, a rough sketch by Civil War illustrator Alfred Waud, and the original Ulke photograph of the death room which appeared in the 1965 *American Heritage.*

The Lincoln deathbed scene was a favorite of Victorian illustrators. Most results were fanciful, featuring far too many political dignitaries of the time crowded around the death bed, as the essay in this publication reveals. Alfred Waud, an illustrator for *Harper's Weekly,* on the scene immediately after the assassination, made sketches of the death room. One of his sketches, furnished and published in *Harper's Weekly,* detailed the furnishings of the death room, with wallpaper, the carpet, and the figures huddled around the bed of the dying president. In an unpublished sketch, Waud rendered the back of the death room, giving views of the room from both ends. Waud's drawings became the basis of the 1978-80 restoration.

Osborn Oldroyd had removed the back wall of the death room to accommodate museum cases. The Park Service replaced the wall in the early 1930s but inaccurately, according to the Waud sketch. We moved the door about 18 inches away from the wall and installed an original 1849 door taken from the third floor of the house. The 1849 door had hardware identical to that in the Waud drawing and was of the appropriate size. We also reproduced the wall clothes rack and the stovepipe on the back wall in the Waud drawing, as well as an S-shaped wall gaslight on the side wall.

Another illustrator, Albert Berghaus, had visited the Petersen House immediately after the assassination and published a drawing of the death bed scene in *Frank*

*Leslie's Illustrated Newspaper.* Appearing with this wood engraving in *Leslie's* was an affidavit signed by most of the boarders of the Petersen House, attesting to its authenticity. Berghaus's drawing confirmed the drawings by Waud and featured the clothes rack and stove pipe.

An account published in *Leslie's* with Berghaus's engraving described the wallpaper in the death room as "a brownish paper, figured with a white design." Both the Berghaus and Waud drawings show a striped wallpaper with a repeat foliated motif and a running border along the top of the walls. The Ulke photograph gave a better picture of the wallpaper, although it was slightly blurred. Using these sources, Scalamandre of New York created a wallpaper for the restoration. The wallpaper pattern that the Park Service had previously used in the room had come from a panel collected by Oldroyd and certified by him as the original death room paper. Park Service architect Gary Thompson found that this panel was actually many layers of paper glued together. The past restoration of the room had erred in reproducing only the top layer, as confirmed by the Ulke photograph. After de-laminating a small sample of the layered paper, the first and lowest level of paper revealed a tiny drab sample of a small repeat floral pattern which was incorporated into the Scalamandre design.

The two parlors and the hallway presented further problems to our restoration since no contemporary drawings or photographs were found to give a clue for their restoration. A floor plan sketch did exist, indicating furniture locations in the parlor, which had been recorded by Major A. F. Rockwell who was reportedly present that fatal night. The gaslight fixtures which the Park Service had hanging in the parlors and hallway for many years proved to be of a later period. Through Craig Littlewood, a 19th century lighting expert, we were able to obtain a set of 1850 gasoliers for the parlors and a pear-shaped single handing fixture of the period for the hallway.

For the refurnishing, John Bruchsch of the Harpers Ferry Historic Furnishings Office of the Park Service collected furniture and personal toilet articles similar to those seen in the Waud and Berghaus drawings of the death room. NPS curator Vera Craig spent years researching the furnishing plan for the house. Period antiques were used instead of reproductions. (Attempts to woo back the original death room furniture from the Chicago Historical Society proved unsuccessful.) The front parlor where Mrs. Lincoln kept her vigil contains a horsehair parlor set which Osborn Oldroyd is reputed to have brought in from the Lincoln home in Springfield, Illinois. The back parlor is presented as a bedroom where Secretary of the Interior John P. Usher slept part of the night, and where Secretary Stanton interviewed visitors.

Although enough evidence exists to make the death room more or less an accurate recreation, the rest of the historic interior is largely conjecture. Highly theatrical wallpaper in the parlors heightens the dramatic effect.

The 1978-80 interior recreation of the house where Lincoln died is an early example of the movement toward dramatic restorations of Victorian interiors during the 1980s and early 1990s, as the historic preservation movement gained momentum and spread. The genre is very familiar now and can be seen in historic houses and bed and breakfasts across the country. However, at the time it was done, the Petersen House restoration represented a reinstated dramatic 19th-century color palette, at a time when design was emerging from the timid colors of modernism. The clutter abhorred by the last generation is back in full view.

# ENDNOTES

1 Fred I. Greenstein, "What the President Means to Americans," James D. Barber, ed., *Choosing the President* (Englewood Cliffs, NJ: Prentice-Hall, 1974), 123.
2 *Ibid.,* 142-143.
3 James W. Clarke, *American Assassins: The Darker Side of Politics* (Princeton: Princeton University Press, 1982), 153 & 262.
4 Dean K. Simonton, *Why Presidents Succeed* (New Haven: Yale University Press, 1987), 185-228. See also, Schlesinger, Arthur, Jr., "The Schlesinger Poll," *The New York Times Magazine,* 15 December 1996.
5 Dorothy Meserve Kunhardt and Philip B. Kunhardt, Jr., *Twenty Days* (New York: Harper & Row, 1965), 46-47.
6 Account of Henry Safford, *Springfield Republican,* 18 February 1917.
7 Kunhardt and Kunhardt, *Twenty Days,* 46-47.
8 W. Emerson Reck, *A Lincoln: His Last 24 Hours* (Columbia: University of South Carolina Press, 1994), 136-148.
9 *Ibid.,* 139-140.
10 See Carl Bersch's painting, *Lincoln Borne By Loving Hands* (1865) in Harold Holzer and Mark E. Neely, Jr., *Mine Eyes Have Seen the Glory: The Civil War in Art* (New York: Orion Books, 1993), 167. The original painting is in The Ford's Theatre Collection.
11 Timothy S. Good, *We Saw Lincoln Shot: One Hundred Eyewitness Accounts* (Jackson: University Press of Mississippi, 1995), 24.
12 Stefan Lorant, *Lincoln: A Picture Story of His Life* (rev. ed., New York: W. W. Norton & Co., 1969), 269.
13 Roy P. Basler et. al., eds., *The Collected Works of Abraham Lincoln,* Roy P. Basler, ed., (8 vols. New Brunswick: Rutgers University Press, 1953-55), 3:29.
14 Leonard, Lesley A., "Abraham Lincoln and the 'Rubber Room,'" *Surratt Courier* XI (1986): 1,8.
15 Copyright records, Southern District of New York, 1865, in the Library of Congress, Rare Book Collection.
16 Frederic A. Conningham, *Currier & Ives Prints: An Illustrated Check List* (rev. ed., New York: Crown Publishers, 1970), v-viii.
17 Good, *We Saw Lincoln Shot,* 26.
18 Kunhardt and Kunhardt, *Twenty Days,* 49.
19 See, for comparison, the prints illustrated side-by-side in Lorant, *Lincoln: A Picture Story of His Life,* 267-269.
20 Kunhardt and Kunhardt, *Twenty Days,* 78.
21 Ritchie's Historical Picture, *Death of President Lincoln* (advertising brochure), (New York: A. H. Ritchie & Co., 1868), 8-9.
22 See *Harper's Weekly* for April, May, June, and July, 1865.
23 David Donald, "Getting Right with Lincoln," *Lincoln Reconsidered* (New York: Alfred A. Knopf, 1956), 4.
24 George Bancroft, *Memorial Address on the Life and Character of Abraham Lincoln* (Washington: Government Printing Office, 1866).
25 Kunhardt and Kunhardt, *Twenty Days,* 80. See also Good, *We Saw Lincoln Shot,* 26.

# ACKNOWLEDGEMENTS

The authors are grateful for the help and encouragement they received from the following individuals and institutions: Dwight Pitcaithely, Chief Historian of the National Park Service, and Michael Maione, Site Historian of the Ford's Theatre National Historic Site; Dr. Gerald Prokopowicz, Historian and Director of Special Projects of the Lincoln Museum in Fort Wayne; Gary Scott, Chief Historian of the National Capitol Region, National Park Service, and Arnold Goldstein, Superintendent, National Capital Parks-Central, National Park Service; Laurie Verge, Historian/Manager of the Surratt House Museum; Joan Chaconas, former president of the Surratt Society; Philip Kunhardt III of Kunhardt Productions; Michael Rhode, Chief Archivist of the National Museum of Health and Medicine of Walter Reed Army Medical Center; Dr. William D. Pederson, Director of American Studies, Louisiana State University - Shreveport; and historian Edward Steers, Jr. We also thank Donna Petorella for expertly typing the manuscript. Special gratitude goes to our editor at Thomas Publications, Sarah C. Rodgers, and to Jim Thomas for his help on production.

✣ ✣ ✣

This monograph is based on a lecture delivered at Ford's Theatre in Washington, D. C., on November 10, 1996, to celebrate the centennial of Federal ownership of the Petersen House.

# ABOUT THE AUTHORS

Harold Holzer has authored, co-authored, and edited eleven books on Lincoln and the Civil War era, including a number of landmark studies of the engravings and lithographs of the period. These books include *The Lincoln Image, Changing the Lincoln Image*, and *The Confederate Image.* His 1993 work, *The Lincoln-Douglas Debates,* inspired the C-SPAN televised re-creations of all seven debates in 1994, for which Holzer served as advisor and frequent on-air commentator. Holzer serves as Vice President for Communications at The Metropolitan Museum of Art.

Frank J. Williams has edited three books on the Lincoln theme, and has led three major national membership organizations devoted to the history of the period: the Abraham Lincoln Association, The Ulysses S. Grant Association, and, currently, The Lincoln Forum. In addition, he is one of the country's leading collectors of Lincolniana, and one of its most popular public speakers on the Lincoln theme. Following a 25-year-long career as an attorney, Williams now serves as Associate Justice of the Rhode Island Superior Court.